A Manual of
Comparative Typography
The PANOSE System

A Manual of Comparative Typography/
The PANOSE System

Benjamin Bauermeister

VNR VAN NOSTRAND REINHOLD COMPANY
New York

To Barb, who taught me to look at letters as shapes; to George, who showed me the beauty in well-crafted form; to M. C. Voertman, for putting the printer's ink in my blood; and to Erica, for putting up with it.

Copyright © 1988 by Van Nostrand Reinhold Company Inc.
Library of Congress Catalog Card Number 87-10483
ISBN 0-442-21187-2

Printed in the United States of America

Illustrations by David Hastings
Typographic coordination by Marcelle Amelia

Van Nostrand Reinhold Company Inc.
115 Fifth Avenue
New York, New York 10003

Van Nostrand Reinhold Company Limited
Molly Millars Lane
Wokingham, Berkshire RG11 2PY, England

Van Nostrand Reinhold
480 La Trobe Street
Melbourne, Victoria 3000, Australia

Macmillan of Canada
Division of Canada Publishing Corporation
164 Commander Boulevard
Agincourt, Ontario M1S 3C7, Canada

16 15 14 13 12 11 10 9 8 7 6 5 4 3 2 1

Library of Congress Cataloging-in-Publication Data
Bauermeister, Benjamin.
    A manual of comparative typography.

    Bibliography: p.
    Includes index.
    1. Type and type-founding.   2. Printing—Specimens.
I. Title.
Z250.B34   1987   686.2'24   87-10483
    ISBN 0-442-21187-2 (pbk.)

Contents

Acknowledgments

Special thanks to those companies that helped supply the type displayed in this book:

The Alphatype Corporation, for their generous donation of the typesetting of the digital CRS samples

Graphic Services in Tacoma, Washington, for their work on the Compugraphic 8400 digital type samples

The Typehouse in Seattle, Washington, for their work on the Linotronic typesetting equipment

INTRODUCTION

Welcome to PANOSE, an exciting new system of typeface classification. PANOSE is the first accessible, informative specimen system. In PANOSE, typeface styles are arranged according to certain style and appearance characteristics. Because the specimen listing is organized by visual characteristics, similar styles are displayed near one another, with their differences noted. Much like a nature guide that enables you to find the name of a particular tree by noting special features of its leaves or bark, PANOSE uses a seven-digit numerical classification system based on features of individual typefaces to help you quickly locate the exact typeface you desire. The 240 display fonts were chosen on the basis of both their popularity and the variety they give to the book. PANOSE also includes a single-feature cross-reference chart for each typeface, which allows you to find similar faces that have only one different feature. Finally, an alphabetical index provides access to the nearly 350 various type families listed in this manual, totaling over 500 individual fonts.

This sourcebook can be used by anyone interested in type, regardless of experience. If you are a student or client, selecting type for the first time or the fiftieth, the PANOSE system can help you locate the style you want, regardless of your knowledge of type names or historical periods. Identify the characteristics of a type style you want, and use the classification index to find it as well as to locate similar fonts. Artists and designers will find PANOSE indispensable for matching an existing typeface or for finding a new variation of an old favorite. Teachers, historians, and professionals will appreciate the natural groupings that occur in PANOSE; families such as single-weight Egyptian, and visually similar groups such as Stressed Sans Serif are on adjacent pages for easy comparison and accurate identification.

USING THIS BOOK

You can locate type specimens in this book in four different ways, depending on what you are looking for and your knowledge of type.

Even with little or no knowledge of typography, you should be able to choose the seven digits concerning serifs, proportion, form, stroke, and other details in order to determine a classification number. Once you have decided on the classification number for the font, look in the Classification Index at the back of this book to find the corresponding display page number where your desired type style is located. With very little practice, you should be able to generate numbers in less than a minute to locate whatever typeface you desire, if it exists. In some instances, the numbers you choose will have no exact match in the Classification Index. In these cases, find the closest number and use the cross-reference chart on the specified page to locate the variation of the displayed font that meets your needs.

The second method of access to the display section is used when you want to match or identify an existing type style. When choosing the number-generating digits, you should usually avoid the options followed by a bullet, which indicates that an option is seldom used and so few faces with it will be available. When matching type, however, it is not necessary to avoid options with bullets; in fact, these bulleted options will usually speed up your matching process. Once you have determined a number based on characteristics, you can find a name for your style and a display page number in the Classification Index. The display page will provide positive identification, as well as a cross-reference chart that lists alternate pages to check in case you have an imperfect match.

For the experienced designer or typographer, the Stylistic Index lists both historical periods and various stylistic families of type by name, along with their corresponding classification and page numbers. Because the type styles are categorized by appearance, most families and historical periods are adjacent in the body of the display section. If, for instance, you are interested in an Egyptian type font, the Stylistic Index will list the areas of the book where the Egyptian styles are found. For an experienced designer or typographer, the Stylistic Index can therefore be even more expedient to use than the number-generating process.

Finally, for the expert typographer who knows all type by name and has less need for an arrangement of type by style, there is the Alphabetical Index. This index lists by name all the fonts displayed in this manual as well as any names referred to in the alternate names section of each display page and provides a corresponding classification and display page number.

There is one more intended use for this book: thumbing through it. It is the least time effective, but if you are not in a hurry, it will provide the greatest educational use of this resource. The list of fonts compiled in this book is vast; many are new designs. Thumbing through, in what used to be the only way to access a specimen book, gives you exposure to new faces and allows you to develop new design application ideas.

USING THE NUMBER GENERATOR

This book classifies a wide range of standard text and display type styles. The following is an explanation of the categories and features used to generate the seven-digit classification number by which the type styles in this book are arranged. These options do not attempt to pinpoint the dimension, size, or weight of a particular typeface; those variations are shown on the display page or surrounding pages in the display section to which the classification number will guide you.

Many of the options provided in the different categories listed below are applicable to only a few type styles and are rarely seen. These options are followed by a bullet and should be avoided in the process of determining a classification number for the font you desire, as you may not find an appropriate type style with the number you specify, simply because no such typeface exists. Usually these options can be explored by using the cross-reference chart once you have located a proper starting page in the display section. Remember, this book can quickly locate a typeface for you, but at this point it cannot design one. Maybe next year.

1. SERIF STYLE

1. Serif   2. Sans Serif

The first decision you must make in selecting a type style is whether or not the design you are looking for has feet, known as *serifs*, and what those serifs look like. *Sans serif* means "without feet." Ten choices are provided for how the serifs, or lack thereof, should appear.

The selection of a serif style will greatly influence the appearance of the type style you choose. It is also the most difficult option set to work through. The choices listed are very general; more minute variations are usually available among the final alphabets found in the display section. It should also be noted that a serif style may change within a single family as the character's weight increases. The PANOSE system uses the serif style of the medium weight to classify the type. The ten choices are:

1. Cove serif
2. Square serif
3. Square cove serif
4. Thin line serif
5. Exaggerated serif •
6. Triangle serif •
7. Square normal end sans serif
8. Square perpendicular end sans serif •
9. Flared end sans serif
0. Rounded end sans serif •

SERIF

1. Cove Serif

1. Cove Serif   1. Cove Serif

The first option for a serif is the *cove serif*, by far the most common of any listed in this book, and it is easy to distinguish. The cove serif is nothing more than a line whose connection to the supporting leg has been softened by the addition of rounded coves to the inside corners.

The cove serifs appear in a great variety of ways. If you are attempting to match a cove serif design, be certain that it fits these three criteria: it is significantly rounded at the inside corners—otherwise it is a triangular serif; its tips come to a point, sharp or dull, yet not flat; and the serif is a striking element of the font's design. The cove serifs may be slightly cusped, dull, short, or long. If the serif is very small, it might be classified as a flared sans serif.

2. Square Serif

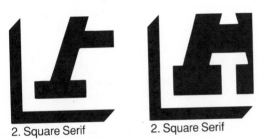

2. Square Serif   2. Square Serif

3. Square Cove Serif

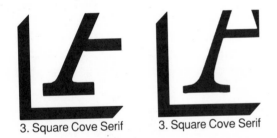

3. Square Cove Serif   3. Square Cove Serif

The *square serif* and its companion, the *square cove*, distinguish a group of type styles known as the Egyptian family. The requirement for classification as a square serif is simple: a square serif must have at least two corners on each serif. The square cove, as you might expect, is a softened version of the strict square serif.

In comparison to other serif styles, the square serif (or slab serif) is the most easily identified. Identification of the square cove is moderately more difficult because of the softening of the connection to the supporting leg. In classifying a square cove serif, be certain that the left and right sides of the serif have a straight, flat appearance; otherwise the serif style might be more similar to a cove serif or even to that of an exaggerated serif.

4. Thin Line Serif

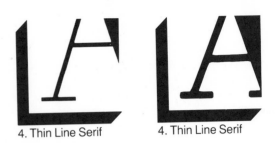

4. Thin Line Serif   4. Thin Line Serif

The *thin line serif* is the modern variation of the cove serif. The major difference between the two is that the thin line serif is not softened at the contact point between the supporting arm and the serif. The thin line serif includes any serif style that is uncoved and light. In some instances the difference between a thin line serif and a square serif is very difficult to distinguish. In these cases the serif is classified according to its weight, the lighter being thin line and the heavier being square.

Both of the serifs illustrated fall into the thin line serif category. If the right-most example of the thin line serif styles were any heavier or more flat-edged it would surely be a square serif.

5. Exaggerated Serif •

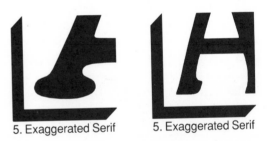

5. Exaggerated Serif   5. Exaggerated Serif

Because of the infinite variety of serif styles, the *exaggerated serif* category is used to classify those styles that do not easily fall into the standard description categories. Included in this category are the very heavy bone-shaped serifs and the strongly cusped designs. In addition to these types, there are also overemphasized and unclassifiable serif styles. Often these fonts are display fonts that border on being classified as decorative.

The serifs shown may meet the requirements of one of the other serif styles, but because of their odd or exaggerated appearance, they are classified in this category.

6. Triangle Serif •

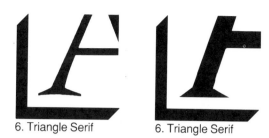

6. Triangle Serif   6. Triangle Serif

Very few fonts incorporate the *triangular serif*. It is a sharp and awkward serif invented by the mind, not the eye. It is most easily seen in the typeface known as Maximal, a popular face, primarily by virtue of its triangular serifs.

Triangular serifs are very rare. Be certain, if you are matching an existing font, that the inside corners are absolutely flat; if they have any curve to them, the font is likely to be classified as having cove serifs.

SANS SERIF

The remaining serif variations describe sans serif letter styles. The sans serif leg-end styles are much easier to classify than the serif styles, mainly because they have much less variation.

7. Square Normal End

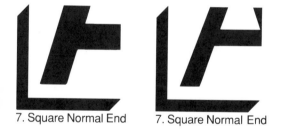

7. Square Normal End   7. Square Normal End

8. Square Perpendicular End •

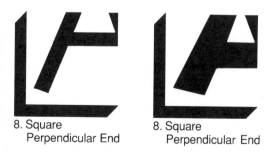

8. Square
Perpendicular End   8. Square
                          Perpendicular End

Sans serif letterforms have primarily two types of leg-end styles: the *square normal* and the *square perpendicular*. The leg ends of the square normal style must either lie flat on the base line or meet it at 90 degrees. The square perpendicular leg ends, on the other hand, must always be at a 90-degree angle to their supporting arm. This is most obvious in diagonal letterforms, such as *A*, *V*, and sometimes *M*. The square perpendicular option is rarely used; thus it is followed by a bullet.

9. Flared End

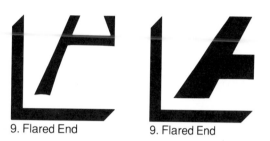

9. Flared End   9. Flared End

The *flared end* style can be easily confused with a small cove serif. Watch for two differences. First, most flared end style serifs start to widen much higher on the supporting leg than do small cove serifs. Second, in a number of contemporary fonts, very minute serifs have been added to what traditionally were sans serif letterforms. In these cases, the serif is classified here as a flared end rather than a small cove because most of these "serifed sans serif" faces, in keeping with other sans serif faces, have little or no contrast within the letterform. See category 3 for a more in-depth description of contrast.

0. Rounded End •

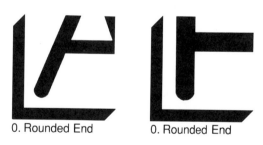

0. Rounded End   0. Rounded End

The *rounded end* is very rare and should be used only to match an existing typeface. Category 0 is used when the leg end is round instead of flat. Moreover, additional fonts have been classified under this option if the overall feeling or color of the letters is rounded. In all, if a font has any rounded corners that are traditionally square in other fonts, it will be classified in this category.

2. PROPORTION

Proportion is not the shape of individual letters; rather, it is their relationship to each other. Proportion is determined by such details as the geometric rules that are used to construct the letters, as well as overall specifications such as condensed and expanded.

The first three proportion categories are the most difficult to identify because they are all subsets of what we would normally call plain letters, in that they are neither condensed or expanded. In these options we see how the geometry of various letterforms works to create a well-balanced alphabet.

1. Old Style

1. Old Style Proportion

2. Modern

2. Modern Proportion

3. Even Width

3. Even Width Proportion

Letter designs throughout history have followed an amazingly straightforward progression with regard to their proportional changes. The early type styles are generally known as *old style*. The proportions of these letters are strictly geometrical;

consequently, the individual letter widths vary greatly. The geometric system by which the letters of this style are constructed is based on the three primary letter shapes: the square, the circle, and the triangle. For example, the letter *O* is formed from a perfect circle, while the letter *S* is formed from two circles placed one on top of another. This results in the *S* being one-half the width of the *O*. The same situation occurs in the square shapes, as demonstrated by the double-shaped letters *F* and *E*. The letter *E* is formed by the stacking of two squares, making it narrow in relation to the single-shaped letters. Letters with triangular shapes have the same characteristic: the construction of the double-triangle *X* is half the width of the single-triangle *V*.

Type designs from the *modern* period lose their strict geometry and become less varied in width. The circular *O* becomes an oval, and the arms of the once narrow letter *E* are elongated to make it more compatible with the single-shape letterforms.

Finally, there is the *even width* category, typified by more contemporary type styles, where letters have been stretched and compressed until they are all of nearly equal width. You can see the return of the strict full-size geometric shapes in letters such as *O* and *V*, while the two-part letters continue to expand, as seen in the letters *E* and *S*. Also included in this category are the fonts that, while neither modern nor condensed, have full-form letters that are slightly taller than they are wide, such as Eurostile and Univers.

4. Expanded

4. Expanded Proportion

Those letters with standard widths greater than the height of the uppercase letters are classified as *expanded*. Expanded letterforms can be easily identified by looking at the capital *O*. If it is a wide oval, the overall dimensions of the characters have been expanded, creating a style of great stability and width.

5. Condensed

5. Condensed Proportion

Condensed letters are the opposites of expanded letters. The condensed option is a little more difficult to judge because no single character can be used to identify it easily, as the O can for expanded fonts. Most often the font name itself will be identified as condensed. In those instances where this is not the case, the uppercase O is again used for reference, although it is difficult to distinguish between a modern and a condensed O, both being ovals. The more exaggerated the oval, the more likely it is that the font is condensed.

6. Monospaced (Typewriter)

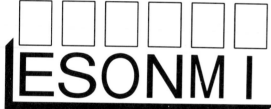

6. Monospaced Proportion

Unlike even width—which has the appearance of even spacing between the letterforms, though the rules are broken for narrow letters like *I* and wide letters like *M*—each letter in a *monospaced* font has the same character width and spacing. Monospaced fonts are also typically known as typewriter fonts because they mimic the letter widths and spacing created by an old-fashioned typewriter. With the advent of modern typesetting, many of these styles became available in various media from hot to digital type, and several were developed into fonts in their own right. Some of these so-called typewriter fonts have dropped their true monospacing in favor of greater legibility; nonetheless, they are classified as monospace because of their typewritten appearance.

3. CONTRAST

Most letters have stems and arms of varying thicknesses; usually the horizontal members are thinner than the vertical. The Contrast category details the relationship between a letter's members, describing the structural contrast between the heavy and the light elements of the individual letterforms. Contrast does *not* have anything to do with the surrounding whiteness of the page or the contrasts among different letters; this category deals only with contrasts in elements of a character. Be careful not to confuse Contrast with weight when examining options here. Once again, the uppercase O acts as a good reference character to determine the contrast of a given font.

The choices you make in this Contrast category will determine which set of options you should look at in the next category, Stroke Variation (4A) or Arm Type (4B). If you choose options 1 through 5 in this category, go to 4A, Stroke Variation. If you choose option 6, go to 4B, Arm Type.

1. Low

Fonts that have *low* contrast are generally those serifed styles with only a very slight variation between the weights of the stems and the arms.

2. Medium Low

Medium low styles show subtle variations in contrast and maintain a very soft appearance. Many of the Old Style fonts will be found in this option, as will the optically refined sans serif fonts, such as Optima and Souvenir Gothic.

3. Medium

Medium contrast is the most common option for serifed fonts. Included in this selection are the myriad of fonts that have good typographical contrast yet are not designed to draw attention to their structural variety.

4. Medium High

Most of the modern fonts have *medium high* contrast, with a visible contrast between the stems and arms of the letters. This contrast is accentuated by the use of equally thin serifs.

5. High

Those fonts that use extreme contrast between stems and arms to create a dramatic effect are the only styles classified as *high* contrast.

6. None

If a type style has no variation in width between the stems and arms of its characters, it is said to be a single-stroke letterform and is classified here as having no contrast. Most of the fonts so classified will be sans serif styles, although many square serif styles are also single stroke. Often when the weight of a font becomes heavy, contrast is increased to provide adequate space for the horizontal arms; this increase in contrast also occurs in the rounded letterforms when they have been altered to increase legibility. Fonts are classified as having no contrast if the medium weight of the font is single stroke in form.

If you have chosen option 6, no contrast, then you will use category 4B to select your fourth digit.

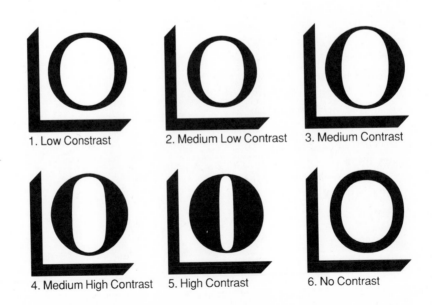

1. Low Contrast   2. Medium Low Contrast   3. Medium Contrast

4. Medium High Contrast   5. High Contrast   6. No Contrast

4A. STROKE VARIATION

This category, used for double-stroke letters, identifies the speed at which a letter's stroke changes width and the direction of stress created by that change. The options for speed are gradual, abrupt, and instant. They are coupled with the options for stress, diagonal, vertical, horizontal, and mixed. These two sets of options are combined and listed below in their historical order, starting with typography's calligraphic beginnings, demonstrated by the diagonal stress and the gradual shifting of letter weight, continuing through the transitional period of mixed stresses, then to the modern period with its abrupt and strictly vertical stress, and finally the more decorative stroke variations of horizontal and instant vertical.

1. Gradual with diagonal stress
2. Gradual with mixed stress •
3. Gradual with vertical stress
4. Gradual with horizontal stress •
5. Abrupt with vertical stress
6. Abrupt with horizontal stress •
7. Instant vertical stress •

Option 2 provides a choice that is fairly rare. During what is known as the transitional period of type design, the stress of the letters changed from diagonal to vertical. Some alphabets designed during this period changed the stress in only the uppercase; the lowercase retained its diagonal stress. Thus, these faces have mixed stress. This option is not only seldom used, it is also often overlooked.

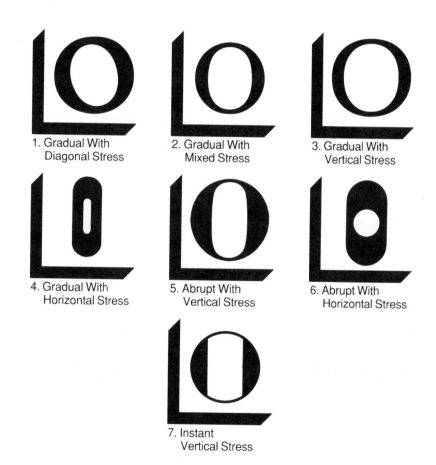

1. Gradual With Diagonal Stress

2. Gradual With Mixed Stress

3. Gradual With Vertical Stress

4. Gradual With Horizontal Stress

5. Abrupt With Vertical Stress

6. Abrupt With Horizontal Stress

7. Instant Vertical Stress

4B. ARM TYPE

To create some distinction among the various single-stroke font styles, this category details two different aspects of letter design. Although most of these options are directed toward sans serif letters, the few single-stroke serif designs that exist will be accommodated as well. The two variations covered here are Arm/Stem style and Round Letter Opening style. Each of the two topics has three variations; they are grouped into nine different options:

1. Straight arms, horizontal opening
2. Bowed arms, horizontal opening •
3. Concave arms, horizontal opening •
4. Straight arms, wedge opening
5. Bowed arms, wedge opening •
6. Concave arms, wedge opening •
7. Straight arms, vertical opening
8. Bowed arms, vertical opening •
9. Concave arms, vertical opening •

The first choice you must make in this category concerns stem and arm style. The definitions are quite simple. *Straight arms* applies to those fonts with arms (especially those of the uppercase *A* and *W*) that remain straight and parallel. Some of the bolder display fonts, which rely on the ability to bend their normally straight arms to compensate for their unwieldy weight, fall into the *bowed arms* option. The final option is for those fonts with *concave* stems and arms. These fonts are easiest to distinguish by evaluating the uppercase *I*, the sides of which will curve inward, rather than being perfectly parallel.

The second set of options defines the angle at which the opening of the uppercase *C* (and consequently the *G* and *S*) is set. See the illustration for an exaggerated display of *horizontal, wedge,* and *vertical* openings. In the horizontal option, the opening is parallel. If either of the opening angles is not horizontal or vertical, then the font has a wedge opening. Sometimes a wedge opening will actually be an inverse wedge. Most of the serifed fonts classifed as single stroke have a vertical opening.

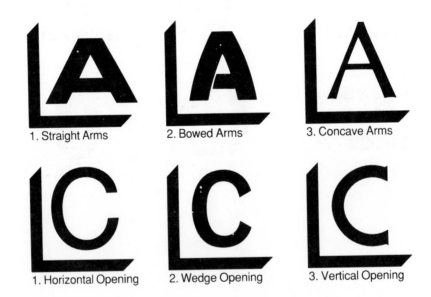

1. Straight Arms   2. Bowed Arms   3. Concave Arms

1. Horizontal Opening   2. Wedge Opening   3. Vertical Opening

5. LETTERFORM

The form of a letter is very important for establishing the mood and appearance of any style. Classification is determined by evaluating the rounded letterforms, such as O and C, for six variations:

1. Contact
2. Boxed •
3. Flattened
4. Rounded •
5. Off center •
6. Square •

The first option, *contact*, is by far the most common: the exterior outline of the form comes in contact with the visual parameters of the letter's dimensions at only four points. Similar is the *boxed* option, in which there is still only one contact point per side, but the overall form of the rounded letters is square. In the *flattened*, or straight-sided, option, the letter will contact the edge of its external parameters for an extended length, thus flattening the sides of the rounded shapes. The top and bottom of the letterform, however, will still contact the dimensional limits at one point. The *rounded* option is provided for those forms that are primarily squares with dull corners, contacting the parameters for extended lengths on all four sides. Similarly, the *square* option is available for completely sharp, square-cornered letterforms. *Off center* forms are predominantly asymmetrical forms. Note that a contact style need not be a true circle: it can be an oval without flat sides.

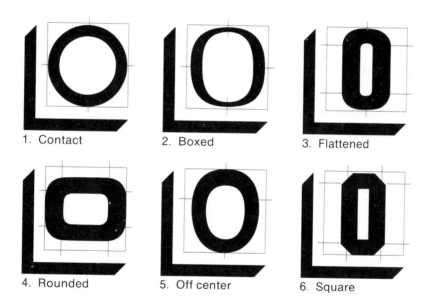

1. Contact   2. Boxed   3. Flattened

4. Rounded   5. Off center   6. Square

6. MIDLINE

The Midline category encompasses two aspects of type design. The first option determines the position of the midline throughout the alphabet. This option offers four choices. These four choices are combined with the second option, which defines whether or not the apexes of pointed letterforms, such as uppercase *A, W,* and *M,* are trimmed flat or remain sharp.

1. Standard midline with trimmed apex
2. Standard midline with pointed apex
3. High standard midline with trimmed apex
4. High standard midline with pointed apex
5. Constant midline with trimmed apex
6. Constant midline with pointed apex
7. Constant low midline with trimmed apex •
8. Constant low midline with pointed apex •

Type designers have handled the midline positions in various ways. *Standard* midline position generally is centered slightly high throughout most of the alphabet, with the exception of the uppercase *A,* which is usually set equally low. A common variation on this standard is to place the midline noticeably higher than average and to drop the

midline of the *A* considerably lower. This style is classified as *high standard.* The last two options, both rather decorative, pertain to those fonts without a variation in the midline of the *A.* These two options apply to fonts that have their midlines entirely set in the middle, *constant midline,* and those that are entirely set low, *constant low midline.* There are also a very few entirely high-set midline positions, which have been classified under the high standard option.

A *trimmed apex* is, it would seem, a very simple concept to visualize: if the top of an uppercase *A* is flat, it is considered trimmed; if it is not flat, it is considered *pointed.* Yet two difficulties arise. First, many sans serif fonts have only a very small flat area, one that is hardly noticeable. Second, some serifed fonts with sharp apexes have right arms that overlap the left arm beneath and to the left of the apex. (For example, see the serifed *A* in the serif style illustration on page ix.) Hence two more rules are added to the determination of the apex trim: to be considered trimmed, the flat area at the top of the letter must be greater than half the width of the wider arm to be considered trimmed, and to be considered pointed, the point at the top of the uppercase *A* must be clean and undisturbed to be considered pointed.

1. Trimmed Apex   2. Pointed Apex

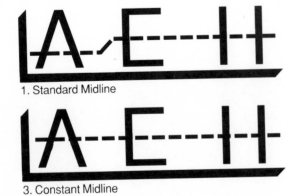

1. Standard Midline

3. Constant Midline

2. Standard High Midline

4. Constant Low Midline

7. x HEIGHT

The x height of a typeface is the height beyond which the bodies of lowercase letters do not extend, generally measured as the height of the lowercase X. The size relationship between uppercase and lowercase letters varies considerably and is an important factor in a style's readability as well as the overall color of a page of typed copy. The four options here are based upon the relationship of the lowercase letters to the uppercase.

1. Small
2. Standard
3. Large
4. All caps

Lowercase letters slightly larger than half the uppercase size are *standard*. Those lowercase letters less than 50 percent of the uppercase height are considered *small*. Lowercase letters taller than 70 percent of the uppercase height are classified as *large*. In many display faces, no lowercase is available, and these are the *all-cap* fonts of option 4.

This concludes the number-generating process. Make sure you have seven digits in your number, and then locate the seven-digit number in the Classification Index. This index will provide a corresponding display page number. If no index number is similar to the classification you have chosen, recheck your number, making sure the digits are in proper order. If they are correct and you still find no similar listing in the Classification Index, choose the closest number available in the index and turn to the corresponding display page. It is often possible to use the cross-reference chart on the display page to find alternate styles of the given type that better fit your needs.

1. Small x Height

2. Standard x Height

3. Large x Height

4. All Caps

USING THE SPECIMEN PAGES

At the top of each specimen page are the font's name and classification number. Below the font name is an alphabet printed in a medium weight (if available). The entire alphabet has been printed vertically down the page so that the page can be folded back for easy comparison with a font on a different page. Red circles are drawn around identifying characteristics of each letter to indicate what makes this style different from others that might share this font's classification number.

In order to demonstrate the appearance of the type style in different weights, the uppercase letters *P, A, N, O, S,* and *E* and the lowercase letters *a, b, e, g, k, m, o, q, s,* and *t* are printed in all available weight variations beneath the classification number. These sixteen letters were selected because they represent the various basic letterforms, making it easy, in conjunction with the full alphabet

listing to the left, to visualize the appearance of the other thirty-six. Beneath each of the display samples is a name label noting the full name of the preceding font.

If an unusual stylistic change occurs because of change in weight, it will either be displayed on the specimen page or a separate classification number will be listed and its specimen page noted above the font information chart. If a type style has companion alphabets, such as condensed or expanded, these variations will usually have separate classification numbers and their specimen pages can be found in the cross-reference chart. If there are not sufficient weight variations in a companion alphabet to warrant a separate specimen page, the variations that do exist will be shown on the same page that displays the roman (noncondensed, nonexpanded) style of the font.

USING THE REFERENCE
INFORMATION

Below each specimen display is a cross-reference chart. When you are selecting a type style, there is often one characteristic that you wish you could alter. You could spend many hours paging through an ordinary specimen book in search of that "just right" style, or you could use the PANOSE cross-reference chart, which directs you to similar type styles if they exist. This chart, at the bottom of each page, offers digit-by-digit variations of the current classification number and lists the corresponding display page numbers of these slightly altered styles. Often the pages listed on the cross-reference chart merely reflect an adequate alternative that is close to the specifications you desire. If, on the other hand, the page listed on the chart is circled in red, this alternate is an identical digit match to your current classification number, with the exception of the single digit for which you have specified a change.

In addition to the cross-reference chart, other information is given about the font in a box above and to the right of the chart. The first information in the box is the name of the vendor who supplied the specimen for the font display. Since some font names are unprotected, many type styles with the same names are slightly altered by different suppliers to suit their needs. Knowing exactly whose font you are looking at can be very handy.

The second line of information contains the type's proposed use as display or text. Often both are plausible uses; the most appropriate use is listed first. Usually this purpose is self-evident.

Similar names are then provided, listing typefaces that are visually related and can be found in different sourcebooks. The listed names are usually less conventional and more ornate. PANOSE does not attempt to classify decorative type styles.

Below the similar-names listing is information on the media for which this font is currently available. Although most hot-type casting methods are no longer used, many unique hot styles are included in this book because digital fonts, which are entering the market at an astonishing rate, are often remakes of popular hot fonts of the past. There is no reason to assume that a popular font will be discontinued because of the changes in typographic technology. Use the information in this list as a minimum listing of the different media currently available. The media included are: hot (including both foundry- and line-casting methods); photo (any method where a film negative font is projected onto light-sensitive paper); dry transfer (adhesive sheets of characters to be pressed onto paste-up boards); digital (fonts held in a computer as geometric formulas and imaged onto light-sensitive paper with a directed laser beam); and bit-mapped (fonts composed of dots on a grid; these fonts are used on both computer monitors and high-resolution laser printers). Concerning the two computer media, digital and bit-mapped, two additional distinctions are noted. PostScript is a new page description language which is capable of very sophisticated type manipulation. Many popular fonts are being converted into this format. These fonts are distinguished by a *PS* in the media listing. Also, Bitstream Inc. has digitizing fonts to create a library of high-quality outline font descriptions. These outlines can be converted into bit-mapped characters for a wide variety of laser printer, digital typesetter, and video applications. These fonts are listed with a *BT*. More popular faces will continue to be reworked as technology advances.

The similar fonts list generally recommends a few fonts which are different in appearance yet similar in feeling to the displayed font. These are often less popular fonts with classification numbers similar to the displayed font, that either were not able to be included in this book or are located on a nonadjacent page.

Also provided is a list of alternate names. These names often reflect fonts that differ only slightly from the shown font. In these cases an abbreviation is given to specify the supplier who uses this alternate name. A listing of the abbreviations for various suppliers precedes the bibliography. Inasmuch as a single font name will vary from supplier to supplier, so too will the alternate names listed in this book. These names are not intended to signify identical styles but rather related ones that could not be displayed.

EXAMPLES

As mentioned earlier, PANOSE can be used in a variety of ways. This section gives two examples of how to apply the PANOSE system. The first demonstrates a standard search for an appropriate typeface, and the second shows how to use PANOSE to match an existing typeface.

SEARCHING FOR A TYPEFACE

Suppose that you know nothing about type styles and have been given the task of selecting a font for a flyer or advertisement; or better yet, you have been given the task of helping a client who knows nothing about type select a font.

You feel that the font needs to be particularly bold to catch the reader's eye, so you decide to look at some sans serif styles. As you ponder the four sans serif options in the first category, you decide to be just a little different, so you choose option 8, perpendicular sans serif, as your first digit. The second digit is not as easy to select; you know that you do not want a condensed or expanded font, but beyond that you are not too certain which proportion scheme will work best. After a moment of hesitation, you decide on option 1, old style, as your second digit since it seems to have the most personality. Since most sans serif font styles are single stroke, you will have a greater variety of fonts to choose from by selecting the no-contrast (single-stroke) option when you select the digit from the Contrast category. Therefore your third digit is a 6. Because you selected a 6 from the Contrast category, you skip category 4A and debate which pair of options from 4B will work best. A review of the digits you have chosen so far indicates that you are selecting a rather standard font. You therefore decide to stay with a straight-armed letter, and you choose a wedge opening to match the perpendicular sans serif you selected in category 1. The next choice is relatively simple. Be-

cause many of the options in the Letterform category are uncommon, as indicated by the bullets, you select option 1, contact, to make certain that you will have a variety of styles from which to choose. Now that you are starting to get a feel for the overall appearance of the font you are selecting, choosing the last two digits will be much easier. In the sixth category, Midline, you decide to follow the angular mood of the font and choose 2, standard midline with pointed apex. Finally, you select a size for the lowercase. Since you want to have good legibility, you opt for a large x height and choose 3.

Your seven-digit classification number is therefore 8164123. When you turn to the Classification Index, you find that the closest font to your number is Syntax, classified as 8164112 and displayed on page 213. When you flip to that page you are delighted to find that the midline position you had originally specified is actually the position of the boldface font. In addition, you notice that this font is available from a variety of suppliers, so you should have no problem ordering it.

MATCHING AN EXISTING TYPEFACE

In this second example we will deal with a usually frustrating problem. You have just been handed an advertisement that your predecessor created just before she was promoted and transferred to an office across the country. You have been instructed to match the type style from the ad so your boss can use it to print some matching napkins for a big open house next month. The last time you did this chore, it took six hours, and by the end of it, you had blisters on both thumbs and all of the fonts looked both exactly the same and completely different, at the same time.

But now you have the PANOSE system, in which all of the similar-looking fonts are grouped together, with pointers showing how they differ. With a sample of the font in front of you, it is easy to pick the digits that correspond to the font you are trying to match. The first digit is obviously a 1, the cove serif option, which is unfortunately the most commonly used serif style available. Undaunted, you proceed onward. The next digit is a little tougher. Because your sample does not have enough letters on it, you cannot tell whether the proportion is old style or even width. Taking a stab in the dark you choose 3 for your second digit, committing yourself to the even width option. The arbitrary nature of the Contrast category slows you down a bit; you decide to pencil in a 2 for medium low contrast. You have much less doubt in your mind about selecting a 3 for category 4A. Your sample definitely has a gradual shift in weight as it moves from thick to thin around the perimeter of the uppercase O, and the thinnest points of the O are directly above one another, giving it a feeling of vertical stress. The Letterform category is more challenging; it is unclear whether the rounded shapes are all perfect circles or slightly boxed, so you jot down the number 2. For the sixth digit you are again a bit uncertain because you do not have a sample of the letter A to judge the midline position. Considering that the rest of the font has been standard in appearance, you choose a 1. The x height is easy to gauge, as the lowercase is almost exactly 60 percent as tall as the uppercase. You jot down the last 2, and your digits are complete. Now you must check if the faces match.

In the Classification Index, you find no exact match for your number 1323212. The closest number to yours is 1321112, ITC Novarese. You turn to that page and realize immediately that something is not quite right. The font on your sample is somehow more dynamic or diverse. You wonder if any font is just like the one displayed, only more classical. You check the cross-reference chart and see that if the second digit, for proportion, were changed from 3, even width, to 1, old style, another face would be a perfect match. You turn to the page listed in the chart and notice the new font, CG Bem, is too classical and too antique. You realize that the problem arose when you neglected to match your fourth digit for arm style, gradual and vertical. Checking the cross-reference chart again, you locate another similar font, and this one, although it is not a perfect match, has a 3 for the fourth digit. When you turn to that page, you notice that there is a red line under the classification number, meaning that there are several fonts with the same number. After comparing the specimens with your sample, you find that Edelweiss matches it exactly.

NUMBER GENERATOR

Typefaces in this book are cataloged by a number that is obtained by selecting options from the following seven categories. Explanations of these options are on pages ix–xix; a review of these explanations may prove useful to anyone using the number-generating process. Keep track of your selected digits on a separate piece of paper. Digits are generated left to right. A classification number followed by a red bullet indicates a rare classification option and should be avoided, unless you are trying to match an existing type.

1. Serif Style
   1 = Cove serif
   2 = Square serif
   3 = Square cove serif
   4 = Thin line serif
   5 = Exaggerated serif •
   6 = Triangle serif •
   7 = Square normal end sans serif
   8 = Square perpendicular end sans serif •
   9 = Flared end sans serif
   0 = Rounded end sans serif •

2. Proportion
   1 = Old style
   2 = Modern
   3 = Even width
   4 = Expanded
   5 = Condensed
   6 = Monospaced

3. Contrast
   1 = Low
   2 = Medium low
   3 = Medium
   4 = Medium high
   5 = High
   6 = None

If you select a typeface with no contrast (6), select from category 4B. If you choose any other contrast level (1–5), use category 4A.

4A. Stroke Variation (double-stroke letters)
   1 = Gradual with diagonal stress
   2 = Gradual with mixed stress •
   3 = Gradual with vertical stress
   4 = Gradual with horizontal stress •
   5 = Abrupt with vertical stress
   6 = Abrupt with horizontal stress •
   7 = Instant vertical stress •

4B. Arm Type (single-stroke letters)
   1 = Straight arms, horizontal opening
   2 = Bowed arms, horizontal opening •
   3 = Concave arms, horizontal opening •
   4 = Straight arms, wedge opening
   5 = Bowed arms, wedge opening •
   6 = Concave arms, wedge opening •
   7 = Straight arms, vertical opening
   8 = Bowed arms, vertical opening •
   9 = Concave arms, vertical opening •

5. Letterform
   1 = Contact
   2 = Boxed •
   3 = Flattened
   4 = Rounded •
   5 = Off center •
   6 = Square •

6. Midline
   1 = Standard midline with trimmed apex
   2 = Standard midline with pointed apex
   3 = High standard midline with trimmed apex
   4 = High standard midline with pointed apex
   5 = Constant midline with trimmed apex
   6 = Constant midline with pointed apex
   7 = Constant low midline with trimmed apex •
   8 = Constant low midline with pointed apex •

7. x Height
    1 = Small
    2 = Standard
    3 = Large
    4 = All caps

S	P	C	A	F	M	X
1	2	3	4	5	6	7

S = Serif Style
P = Proportion
C = Contrast
A = Stroke Variation/Arm Type and Opening
F = Letterform
M = Midline Height and Apex
X = x Height

Proceed to the Classification Index to find the corresponding display page number for your new classification number.

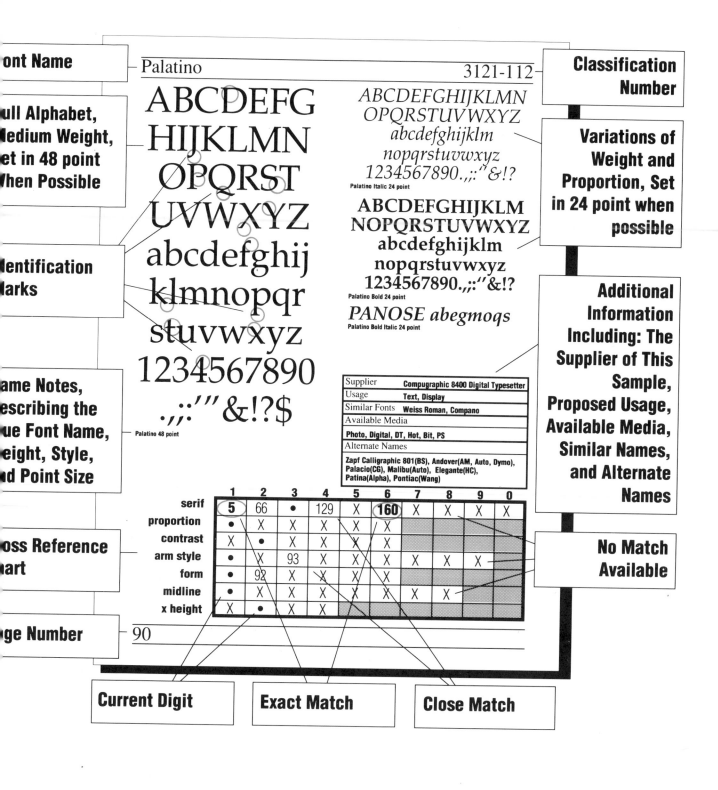

ont Name

ull Alphabet, Medium Weight, et in 48 point When Possible

entification Marks

ame Notes, escribing the ue Font Name, eight, Style, d Point Size

oss Reference art

ge Number

Palatino 3121-112

ABCDEFG
HIJKLMN
OPQRST
UVWXYZ
abcdefghij
klmnopqr
stuvwxyz
1234567890
.,;:'"&!?$

Palatino 48 point

ABCDEFGHIJKLMN
OPQRSTUVWXYZ
abcdefghijklm
nopqrstuvwxyz
1234567890.,;:'"&!?

Palatino Italic 24 point

ABCDEFGHIJKLM
NOPQRSTUVWXYZ
abcdefghijklm
nopqrstuvwxyz
1234567890.,;:'"&!?

Palatino Bold 24 point

PANOSE abegmoqs

Palatino Bold Italic 24 point

Supplier	Compugraphic 8400 Digital Typesetter
Usage	Text, Display
Similar Fonts	Weiss Roman, Compano
Available Media	
Photo, Digital, DT, Hot, Bit, PS	
Alternate Names	
Zapf Calligraphic 801(BS), Andover(AM, Auto, Dymo), Palacio(CG), Malibu(Auto), Elegante(HC), Patina(Alpha), Pontiac(Wang)	

	1	2	3	4	5	6	7	8	9	0
serif	5	66	•	129	X	160	X	X	X	X
proportion	•	X	X	X	X	X				
contrast	X	•	X	X	X	X				
arm style	•	X	93	X	X	X	X	X	X	
form	•	92	X	X	X	X				
midline	•	X	X	X	X	X	X	X		
x height	X	•	X	X						

90

Classification Number

Variations of Weight and Proportion, Set in 24 point when possible

Additional Information Including: The Supplier of This Sample, Proposed Usage, Available Media, Similar Names, and Alternate Names

No Match Available

Current Digit

Exact Match

Close Match

PANOSE
Display Pages

ABCDEFGH IJKLMNOP QRSTUVW XYZ abcdefg hijklmnopqr stuvwxyz 1234567890 .,;'"&!?$

Brewer Text Medium 48 point

ABCDEFGHIJKLMNOP QRSTUVWXYZ abcdefg hijklmnopqrstuvwxyz 1234567890.,;'"&!?$

Brewer Text Light 24 point

ABCDEFGHIJKLMNOP QRSTUVWXYZ abcdef ghijklmnopqrstuvwxyz 1234567890.,;'"&!?$

Brewer Text Bold 24 point

PANOSE abegmoqst

Brewer Text Demibold 24 point

Supplier	Alphatype CRS Digital Typesetter
Usage	**Display, Text**
Similar Fonts	
Available Media	
Photo, Digital	
Alternate Names	
Bauer Text	

	1	2	3	4	5	6	7	8	9	0
serif	●	X	X	X	(149)	X	X	X	216	X
proportion	●	X	52	X	X	X				
contrast	●	4	29	X	X	X				
arm style	●	X	2	X	X	X	X	X	X	
form	●	X	X	X	X	X				
midline	X	X	X	X	X	●	X	X		
x height	X	●	X	X						

ABCDEFG
HIJKLMNO
PQRSTUV
WXYZ abcd
efghijklmno
pqrstuvwxy
1234567
890.,;"&!?$

ITC Weidemann Medium 48 point

PANOSE abegmoqst

ITC Weidemann Book 24 point

PANOSE abegmoqst

ITC Weidemann Book Italic 24 point

PANOSE abegmoqst

ITC Weidemann Medium Italic 24 point

PANOSE abegmoqst

ITC Weidemann Black 24 point

PANOSE abegmoqst

ITC Weidemann Black Italic 24 point

PANOSE abegmoqst

ITC Weidemann Bold 24 point

PANOSE abegmoqst

ITC Weidemann Bold Italic 24 point

Supplier	**Alphatype CRS Digital Typesetter**
Usage	**Text, Display**
Similar Fonts	**Meridien**
Available Media	
Photo, Digital	
Alternate Names	

	1	2	3	4	5	6	7	8	9	0
serif	•	65	89	X	X	X	X	X	X	X
proportion	•	X	X	X	X	X				
contrast	•	23	31	35	X	X				
arm style	X	X	•	X	X	X	X	X	X	
form	•	X	X	X	X	X				
midline	•	X	③	X	X	X	X	X		
x height	X	X	•	X						

2

ABCDEFGH IJKLMNOP QRSTUVW XYZ abcdef ghijklmnop qrstuvwxyz 1234567 890.,;"&!?$

ITC Usherwood Medium 48 point

PANOSE abegmoqst

ITC Usherwood Book 24 point

PANOSE abegmoqst

ITC Usherwood Book Italic 24 point

PANOSE abegmoqst

ITC Usherwood Medium Italic 24 point

PANOSE abegmoqst

ITC Usherwood Bold 24 point

PANOSE abegmoqst

ITC Usherwood Bold Italic 24 point

PANOSE abegmoqst

ITC Usherwood Black 24 point

PANOSE abegmoqst

ITC Usherwood Black Italic 24 point

Supplier	Alphatype CRS Digital Typesetter
Usage	**Text, Display**
Similar Fonts	
Available Media	
Photo, Digital	
Alternate Names	

	1	2	3	4	5	6	7	8	9	0
serif	●	65	89	X	X	X	X	X	X	X
proportion	●	X	X	X	X	X				
contrast	●	26	31	35	X	X				
arm style	X	X	●	X	X	X	X	X	X	
form	●	X	X	X	X	X				
midline	②	X	●	X	X	X	X	X		
x height	X	X	●	X						

ABCDEFG
HIJKLMN
OPQRSTU
VWXYZ
abcdefghijkl
mnopqrstuv
wxyz
1234567890
.,;:''&!?$

Simoncini Garamond 44 point

ABCDEFGHIJKLMN
OPQRSTUVWXYZ
abcdefghijklmnopqrstu
vwxyz
1234567890.,;:''&!?$

Simoncini Garamond Italic 24 point

ABCDEFGHIJKLM
NOPQRSTUVWXYZ
abcdefghijklmnopqrst
uvwxyz
1234567890.,;:''&!?$

Simoncini Garamond Bold 24 point

Supplier	Linotype 202 Digital Typesetter
Usage	**Text**
Similar Fonts	Garamond Stempel
Available Media	
Hot, Photo, Digital	
Alternate Names	

	1	2	3	4	5	6	7	8	9	0
serif	●	66	90	**129**	X	160	X	X	X	X
proportion	●	38	53	X	60	X				
contrast	X	●	29	X	X	X				
arm style	●	22	23	X	X	X	X	X	X	
form	●	X	X	X	X	X				
midline	●	9	X	X	X	X	X	X		
x height	●	5	8	X						

ABCDEFGH IJKLMNOP QRSTUVWX YZ abcdefghijkl mnopqr stuvwxyz 1234567890.,; :'"&!?$

CG Bem Medium 36 point

PANOSE abegmoqst

CG Bem 24 point

PANOSE abegmoqst

CG Bem Italic 24 point

PANOSE abegmoqst

CG Bem Medium Italic 24 point

PANOSE abegmoqst

CG Bem Bold 24 point

PANOSE abegmoqst

CG Bem Bold Italic 24 point

PANOSE abegmoqst

CG Bem Black 24 point

PANOSE abegmoqst

CG Bem Black Italic

Supplier	Compugraphic 8400 Digital Typesetter
Usage	Text, Display
Similar Fonts	Aldus
Available Media	
Photo, Digital	
Alternate Names	
Bembo(Merg), Griffo(Alpha)	

	1	2	3	4	5	6	7	8	9	0
serif	•	(66)	(90)	129	X	(160)	X	X	X	X
proportion	•	38	(53)	X	60	X				
contrast	X	•	(29)	X	X	X				
arm style	•	22	23	X	X	X	X	X	X	
form	•	(20)	X	X	X	X				
midline	•	(13)	(15)	(17)	(19)	X	X	X		
x height	(4)	•	(8)	X						

ABCDEFGHI
JKLMNOP
QRSTUVWX
YZ
abcdefghijkl
mnopqr
stuvwxyz
1234567890.,;
:''&!?$

Garth Graphic 36 Point

ABCDEFGHIJKLMN
OPQRSTUVWXYZ
abcdefghijklmnopqrst
uvwxyz
1234567890.,;:''&!?$

Garth Graphic Italic 24 point

PANOSE abegmoqst

Garth Graphic Bold 24 point

PANOSE abegmoqst

Garth Graphic Bold Italic 24 point

PANOSE abegmoqst

Garth Graphic Extra Bold 24 point

PANOSE abegmoqst

Garth Graphic Black 24 point

Supplier	**Compugraphic 8400 Digital Typesetter**
Usage	**Text, Display**
Similar Fonts	**Centaur**
Available Media	
Photo, Digital	
Alternate Names	

	1	2	3	4	5	6	7	8	9	0
serif	•	(66)	(90)	129	X	(160)	X	X	X	X
proportion	•	38	(53)	X	60	X				
contrast	X	•	(29)	X	X	X				
arm style	•	22	23	X	X	X	X	X	X	
form	•	(20)	X	X	X	X				
midline	•	(13)	(15)	(17)	(19)	X	X	X		
x height	(4)	•	(8)	X						

ABCDEFGHI
JKLMNOP
QRSTUVWX
YZ
abcdefghijklm
nopqr
stuvwxyz
1234567890.,
;:"&!?$

Sabon Roman 36 point

ABCDEFGHIJKLMN
OPQRSTUVWXYZ
abcdefghijklmnopqrst
uvwxyz
1234567890.,;:"&!?$

Sabon Italic 23 point

ABCDEFGHIJKLMN
OPQRSTUVWXYZ
abcdefghijklmnopqrst
uvwxyz
1234567890.,;:"&!?$

Sabon Bold Roman 23 point

Supplier	**Compugraphic 8400 Digital Typesetter**
Usage	**Text**
Similar Fonts	**Berner, September**
Available Media	
Hot, Photo, Bit, Digital	
Alternate Names	
Aldine 421(BS), Sybil(Auto), Sabon-Antiqua(Alpha)	

	1	2	3	4	5	6	7	8	9	0
serif	•	(66)	(90)	129	X	(160)	X	X	X	X
proportion	•	38	(53)	X	60	X				
contrast	X	•	(29)	X	X	X				
arm style	•	22	23	X	X	X	X	X	X	
form	•	(20)	X	X	X	X				
midline	•	(13)	(15)	(17)	(19)	X	X	X		
x height	(4)	•	(8)	X						

ABCDEFGHI JKLMNOP QRSTUVWX YZ abcdefghijkl mnopqr stuvwxyz 1234567890.,; :''&!?$

Administer Book 36 point

ABCDEFGHIJKLMN
OPQRSTUVWXYZ
abcdefghijklmnopqrs
tuvwxyz
1234567890.,;:''&!?$

Administer Light 24 point

*ABCDEFGHIJKLMN
OPQRSTUVWXYZ
abcdefghijklmnopqrstu
vwxyz
1234567890.,;:''&!?$*

Administer Light Italic 24 point

PANOSE abegmoqst

Administer Book Italic 24 point

PANOSE abegmoqst

Administer Bold 24 point

Supplier	**Compugraphic 8400 Digital Typesetter**
Usage	**Text, Display**
Similar Fonts	
Available Media	
Photo, Digital	
Alternate Names	

	1	2	3	4	5	6	7	8	9	0
serif	•	66	90	129	X	160	X	X	X	X
proportion	•	38	53	X	60	X				
contrast	X	•	29	X	X	X				
arm style	•	22	23	X	X	X	X	X	X	
form	•	X	X	X	X	X				
midline	•	X	(16)	(18)	X	X	X	X		
x height	(4)	(5)	•	X						

ABCDEFGHI JKLMNOP QRSTUVWX YZ abcdefghijklm nopqr stuvwxyz 1234567890.,;: ''&!?$

Artcraft Light 36 point

ABCDEFGHIJKLMN OPQRSTUVWXYZ abcdefghijklmnopqrst uvwxyz 1234567890.,;:''&!?$

Artcraft Light Italic 23 point

ABCDEFGHIJKLMN OPQRSTUVWXYZ abcdefghijklmnopqrst uvwxyz 1234567890.,;:''&!?$

Artcraft Bold 23 point

Supplier	**Compugraphic 8400 Digital Typesetter**
Usage	**Display, Text**
Similar Fonts	
Available Media	
Photo, Digital	
Alternate Names	

	1	2	3	4	5	6	7	8	9	0
serif	●	66	90	129	X	160	X	X	X	X
proportion	●	38	53	X	60	X				
contrast	X	●	30	X	X	X				
arm style	●	22	23	X	X	X	X	X	X	
form	●	(21)	X	X	X	X				
midline	(4)	●	X	X	X	X	X	X		
x height	●	(13)	X	X						

ABCDEFG
HIJKLMN
OPQRSTU
VWXYZ

abcdefghijk
lmnopqrst
uvwxyz
123456789
0.,;:"&!?$

Berling Semibold 48 point

ABCDEFGHIJKLMN
OPQRSTUVWXYZ
abcdefghijklmnopqrstu
vwxyz
1234567890.,;:"&!?$
Berling Italic 24 point

ABCDEFGHIJKLMN
OPQRSTUVWXYZ
abcdefghijklmnopqrst
uvwxyz
1234567890.,;:"&!?$
Berling 24 point

PANOSE abegmoqst
Berling Semibold Italic 24 point

Supplier	**Alphatype CRS Digital Typesetter**
Usage	**Text**
Similar Fonts	
Available Media	
Hot, Photo, Digital, DT	
Alternate Names	

	1	2	3	4	5	6	7	8	9	0
serif	●	66	90	129	X	160	X	X	X	X
proportion	●	38	53	X	60	X				
contrast	X	●	30	X	X	X				
arm style	●	22	23	X	X	X	X	X	X	
form	●	(21)	X	X	X	X				
midline	(4)	●	X	X	X	X	X	X		
x height	●	(13)	X	X						

ABCDEF GHIJKLM NOPQRST UVWXYZ abcdefghijk lmnopqrstu vwxyz 1234567 89 0.,;:''&!?$

Eldorado Medium 48 point

PANOSEabegmoqst

Eldorado 24 point

PANOSEabegmoqst

Eldorado Italic 24 point

PANOSEabegmoqst

Eldorado Medium Italic 24 point

PANOSEabegmoqst

Eldorado Bold 24 point

PANOSEabegmoqst

Eldorado Bold Italic 24 point

PANOSEabegmoqst

Eldorado Extra Bold 24 point

PANOSEabegmoqst

Eldorado Extra Bold Italic 24 point

Supplier	Linotype 300 Laser Typesetter
Usage	Text, Display
Similar Fonts	Aeterna
Available Media	
Hot, Photo, Digital	
Alternate Names	

	1	2	3	4	5	6	7	8	9	0
serif	•	66	90	129	X	160	X	X	X	X
proportion	•	38	53	X	60	X				
contrast	X	•	30	X	X	X				
arm style	•	22	23	X	X	X	X	X	X	
form	•	(21)	X	X	X	X				
midline	(4)	•	X	X	X	X	X	X		
x height	•	(13)	X	X						

ABCDEFG HIJKLMN OPQRSTU VWXYZ abcdefghijkl mnopqrstuv wxyz 1234567890 .,;:'"&!?$

Stempel Garamond 42 point

ABCDEFGHIJKLMN OPQRSTUVWXYZ abcdefghijklmnopqrstu vwxyz 1234567890.,;:'"&!?$

Stempel Garamond Italic 22 point

ABCDEFGHIJKLMN OPQRSTUVWXYZ abcdefghijklmnopqrst uvwxyz 1234567890.,;:'"&!?$

Stempel Garamond Bold 22 point

PANOSE abegmoqst

Stempel Garamond Italic Bold 24 point

Supplier	Linotype 202 Digital Typesetter
Usage	Text, Display
Similar Fonts	Garamond Simoncini
Available Media	
Hot, Photo, Digital, Bit	
Alternate Names	
Aldine 525(BS)	

	1	2	3	4	5	6	7	8	9	0
serif	•	66	90	129	X	160	X	X	X	X
proportion	•	38	53	X	60	X				
contrast	X	•	30	X	X	X				
arm style	•	22	23	X	X	X	X	X	X	
form	•	(21)	X	X	X	X				
midline	(4)	•	X	X	X	X	X	X		
x height	•	(13)	X	X						

ABCDEFG
HIJKLMN
OPQRSTU
VWXYZ
abcdefghijkl
mnopqrstuv
wxyz 12345
67890.,;'
&!?$

Goudy Old Style 48 point

ABCDEFGHIJKLMNO
PQRSTUVWXYZ
abcdefghijklmnopqr
stuvwxyz
1234567890.,;'&!?$

Goudy Old Style Italic 24 point

ABCDEFGHIJKLM
NOPQRSTUVWXY
abcdefghijklmnopq
rstuvwxyz
1234567890.,;'&!?$

Goudy Bold 24 point

PANOSE abegmoqst

Goudy Extra Bold 24 point

Supplier	Alphatype CRS Digital Typesetter
Usage	Text
Similar Fonts	Granjon, Goudy Thirty
Available Media	
Digital, Photo, Hot, DT, Bit, PS	
Alternate Names	
Goudy Light(Dymo), Grecian(Wang), Venetian 521(BS)	

	1	2	3	4	5	6	7	8	9	0
serif	●	66	90	129	X	160	X	X	X	X
proportion	●	38	53	X	60	X				
contrast	X	●	30	X	X	X				
arm style	●	22	⟨23⟩	X	X	X	X	X	X	
form	●	X	X	X	X	X				
midline	⟨5⟩	●	⟨15⟩	⟨17⟩	⟨19⟩	X	X	X		
x height	⟨9⟩	●	X	X						

ABCDEFG
HIJKLMN
OPQRSTU
VWXYZ
abcdefghijk
lmnopqrstu
vwxyz
123456789
0.,;:''&!?$

Simoncini Life Roman 42 point

ABCDEFGHIJKLMN
OPQRSTUVWXYZ
abcdefghijklmnopqrst
uvwxyz
1234567890.,;:''&!?$

Simoncini Life Italic 24 point

ABCDEFGHIJKLMN
OPQRSTUVWXYZ
abcdefghijklmnopqrst
uvwxyz
1234567890.,;:''&!?$

Simoncini Life Bold 23 point

Supplier	Linotronic 202 Digital Typesetter
Usage	Text, Display
Similar Fonts	Westminister
Available Media	
Hot, Photo, Digital	
Alternate Names	

	1	2	3	4	5	6	7	8	9	0
serif	●	66	90	129	X	160	X	X	X	X
proportion	●	38	53	X	60	X				
contrast	X	●	30	X	X	X				
arm style	●	22	(23)	X	X	X	X	X	X	
form	●	X	X	X	X	X				
midline	(5)	●	(15)	17	(19)	X	X	X		
x height	(9)	●	X	X						

ABCDEFG
HIJKLMN
OPQRSTU
VWXYZ
abcdefghij
klmnopqrs
tuvwxyz
12345678
90.,;:''&!?$

Expert 48 point

ABCDEFGHIJKLMNO
PQRSTUVWXYZ
abcdefghijklmnopqr
stuvwxyz
1234567890.,;:''&!?$

Expert Italic 24 point

PANOSEabegmoqst

Expert Light 24 point

PANOSEabegmoqst

Expert Light Italic 24 point

PANOSEabegmoqst

Expert Bold 24 point

PANOSEabegmoqst

Expert Black 24 point

Supplier	Linotype 300 Laser Typesetter
Usage	**Text, Display**
Similar Fonts	
Available Media	
Hot, Photo, Digital	
Alternate Names	

	1	2	3	4	5	6	7	8	9	0
serif	•	66	91	**130**	X	160	X	X	X	X
proportion	•	38	53	X	60	X				
contrast	X	•	29	X	X	X				
arm style	•	22	26	X	X	X	X	X	X	
form	•	X	X	X	X	X				
midline	5	13	•	17	19	X	X	X		
x height	X	•	16	X						

ABCDEFG
HIJKLMN
OPQRSTU
VWXYZ
abcdefghi
jklmnopq
rstuvwxyz
1234567
890.,;'&!?

ITC Benguiat Medium 48 point

ABCDEFGHIJKLMN
OPQRSTUVWXYZ
abcdefghijklmnopq
rstuvwxyz 12345
67890.,;'&!?$

ITC Benguiat Medium Italic 24 point

PANOSE abegmoqst

ITC Benguiat Book 24 point

PANOSE abegmoqst

ITC Benguiat Book Italic 24 point

PANOSE abegmoq

ITC Benguiat Bold 24 point

PANOSE abegmoq

ITC Benguiat Bold Italic 24 point

Supplier	**Alphatype CRS Digital Typesetter**
Usage	**Display, Text**
Similar Fonts	**Richmond**
Available Media	
Digital, Photo, DT, Bit, PS	
Alternate Names	
Revival 832(BS)	

	1	2	3	4	5	6	7	8	9	0
serif	•	66	(91)	130	X	160	X	X	X	X
proportion	•	(38)	53	X	(60)	X				
contrast	X	•	29	X	X	X				
arm style	•	22	26	X	X	X	X	X	X	
form	•	X	X	X	X	X				
midline	(8)	X	•	(18)	X	X	X	X		
x height	X	(15)	•	X						

ABCDEFGHIJ KLMNOP QRSTUVWX YZ
abcdefghijklmn opqr stuvwxyz 1234567890.,;: ''&!?$

Kennerly 36 point

ABCDEFGHIJKLMN OPQRSTUVWXYZ abcdefghijklmnopqrstuv wxyz 1234567890.,;:''&!?$

Kennerly Italic 24 point

ABCDEFGHIJKLMN OPQRSTUVWXYZ abcdefghijklmnopqrst uvwxyz 1234567890.,;:''&!?$

Kennerly Bold 22 point

PANOSE abegmoqst

Kennerly Bold Italic 24 point

Supplier	Compugraphic 8400 Digital Typesetter
Usage	**Text, Display**
Similar Fonts	
Available Media	
Photo, Digital, Hot	
Alternate Names	
Kenntonian(HC), Kensington(Auto), LSE Kennerley, Kentuckian(Alpha), Kennerly Old Style(CG)	

	1	2	3	4	5	6	7	8	9	0
serif	•	66	90	129	X	160	X	X	X	X
proportion	•	38	53	X	60	X				
contrast	X	•	29	X	X	X				
arm style	•	22	(27)	X	X	X	X	X	X	
form	•	X	X	X	X	X				
midline	(5)	(13)	(15)	•	(19)	X	X	X		
x height	X	•	(18)	X						

ABCDEFGHI
JKLMNOP
QRSTUVW
XYZ
abcdefghijkl
mnopqr
stuvwxyz
12345678
90.,;:''&!?$

Musketeer Regular 42 point

ABCDEFGHIJKLMNOPQ
RSTUVWXYZ
abcdefghijklmnopqrstuvw
xyz
1234567890.,;:''&!?$

Musketeer Light 22 point

ABCDEFGHIJKLMNOP
QRSTUVWXYZ
abcdefghijklmnopqrstu
vwxyz
1234567890.,;:''&!?$

Musketeer Demibold 21 point

PANOSE abegmoqst

Musketeer Extrabold 24 point

Supplier	**Compugraphic 8400 Digital Typesetter**
Usage	**Display, Text**
Similar Fonts	**Windsor, Della Robbia**
Available Media	
Photo, Digital	
Alternate Names	

	1	2	3	4	5	6	7	8	9	0
serif	●	66	90	129	X	160	X	X	X	X
proportion	●	38	53	X	60	X				
contrast	X	●	29	X	X	X				
arm style	●	22	27	X	X	X	X	X	X	
form	●	X	X	X	X	X				
midline	(8)	X	(16)	●	X	X	X	X		
x height	X	(17)	●	X						

ABCDEFG HIJKLMN O PQRSTUV WXYZ abcd efghijklmnop qrstuvwxyz 1234567890 .,;'"&!?$

Griffo 48 point

ABCDEFGHIJKLMNO PQRSTUVWXYZ abcdefghijklmnopqrstu vwxyz 1234567890.,;:"&!?$

Griffo Italic 24 point

ABCDEFGHIJKLMN OPQRSTUVWXYZ abcdefghijklmnopqrstu vwxyz 1234567890 .,;'"&!?$

Griffo Bold 24 point

PANOSE abegmoqst
Griffo Bold Italic 24 point

Supplier	Alphatype CRS Digital Typesetter
Usage	**Text, Display**
Similar Fonts	
Available Media	
Digital, Photo, DT, Bit	
Alternate Names	
Aldine 401(BS), Aldine Roman(IBM), Bem(CG), Bembo(Merg)	

	1	2	3	4	5	6	7	8	9	0
serif	●	66	90	129	X	160	X	X	X	X
proportion	●	38	53	X	60	X				
contrast	X	●	29	X	X	X				
arm style	●	22	23	X	X	X	X	X	X	
form	●	X	X	X	X	X				
midline	⦶5⦶	⦶13⦶	⦶15⦶	⦶17⦶	●	X	X	X		
x height	X	●	X	X						

ABCDEFG HIJKLMN OPQRSTU VWXYZ

abcdefghijk lmnopqrst uvwxyz 123456789 0.,;:"&!?$

Poppl-Pontifex Medium 48 point

ABCDEFGHIJKLMNO PQRSTUVWXYZ abcdefghijklmnopqrstu vwxyz 1234567890.,;:"&!?$

Poppl-Pontifex Italic 24 point

PANOSE abegmoqst

Poppl-Pontifex 24 point

PANOSE abegmoqst

Poppl-Pontifex Bold 24 point

Supplier	Alphatype CRS Digital Typesetter
Usage	Display, Text
Similar Fonts	Berling
Available Media	
Photo, Digital	
Alternate Names	

	1	2	3	4	5	6	7	8	9	0
serif	•	67	92	129	X	160	X	X	X	X
proportion	•	38	53	X	60	X				
contrast	X	•	29	X	X	X				
arm style	•	22	23	X	X	X	X	X	X	
form	5	•	X	X	X	X				
midline	•	X	X	X	X	X	X	X		
x height	X	•	X	X						

ABCDEFG
HIJKLMN
OPQRSTU
VWXYZ
abcdefghijk
lmnopqrstu
vwxyz
123456789
0.,;:"&!?$

Aldus 48 point

ABCDEFGHIJ
KLMNOPQRS
TUVWXYZ
abcdefghijklmn
opqrstuvwxyz
1234567890.,;:
"&!?$

Aldus Italic 36 point

Supplier	Linotype 202 Digital Typesetter
Usage	Text, Display
Similar Fonts	Bembo
Available Media	
Hot, Photo, Digital	
Alternate Names	

	1	2	3	4	5	6	7	8	9	0
serif	●	67	92	129	X	160	X	X	X	X
proportion	●	38	53	X	60	X				
contrast	X	●	29	X	X	X				
arm style	●	22	23	X	X	X	X	X	X	
form	9	●	X	X	X	X				
midline	X	●	X	X	X	X	X	X		
x height	●	X	X	X						

ABCDEFGHI JKLMNOP QRSTUVWX YZ abcdefghijklm nopqr stuvwxyz 1234567890.,;: ''&!?$

Collage 36 point

ABCDEFGHIJKLMN OPQRSTUVWXYZ abcdefghijklmnopqrstuvw xyz 1234567890,,;:''&?!?$

Collage Italic 24 point

PANOSE abegmoqst

Collage Bold 24 point

PANOSE abegmoqst

Collage Bold Italic 24 point

PANOSE abegmoqst

Collage Black 24 point

PANOSE abegmoqst

Collage Black Italic 24 point

Supplier	**Compugraphic 8400 Digital Typesetter**
Usage	**Text, Display**
Similar Fonts	
Available Media	
Photo, Digital	
Alternate Names	

	1	2	3	4	5	6	7	8	9	0
serif	●	X	X	X	X	X	X	X	X	X
proportion	●	X	X	X	X	X				
contrast	X	●	X	X	X	X				
arm style	15	●	26	X	X	X	X	X	X	
form	●	X	X	X	X	X				
midline	X	X	●	X	X	X	X	X		
x height	●	X	X	X						

ABCDEFG HIJKLMN OPQRSTU VWXYZ abcdefghijkl mnopqrstuv wxyz 12345 67890.,;'&!?

Edelweiss 48 point

ABCDEFGHIJKLMNO PQRSTUVWXYZ abcdefghijklmnopq rstuvwxyz 1234567890.,;"&!?$

Edelweiss Italic 24 point

ABCDEFGHIJKLMN OPQRSTUVWXYZ abcdefghijklmnopq rstuvwxyz 1234567890.,;"&!?$

Edelweiss Extra Bold 24 point

PANOSE abegmoqst

Edelweiss Bold 24 point

Supplier	Alphatype CRS Digital Typesetter
Usage	Text, Display
Similar Fonts	Elmont
Available Media	
Photo, Digital, Hot, DT	
Alternate Names	
Weiss(CG), Weiss Roman(Merg)	

	1	2	3	4	5	6	7	8	9	0
serif	●	68	93	X	X	X	(168)	X	(219)	X
proportion	●	(39)	X	X	X	X				
contrast	2	●	(31)	35	X	X				
arm style	(13)	22	●	X	X	X	X	X	X	
form	●	X	X	X	X	X				
midline	X	●	X	(27)	X	(28)	X	X		
x height	X	●	X	X						

ABCDEFG
HIJKLMN
OPQRSTU
VWXYZ
abcdefghijkl
mnopqrstuv
wxyz
1234567890.,
;:'"&!?$

Granjon 44 point

ABCDEFGHIJKLMNO
PQRSTUVWXYZ
abcdefghijklmnopqrstuv
wxyz
1234567890.,;:'"&!?$

Granjon Italic 24 point

ABCDEFGHIJKLMN
OPQRSTUVWXYZ
abcdefghijklmnopqrstu
vwxyz
1234567890.,;:'"&!?$

Granjon Bold 24 point

Supplier	**Linotronic 202 Digital Typesetter**
Usage	**Text**
Similar Fonts	
Available Media	
Photo, Digital, Hot, Bit	
Alternate Names	
Aldine 424(BS)	

	1	2	3	4	5	6	7	8	9	0
serif	•	68	93	X	X	X	(168)	X	(219)	X
proportion	•	(39)	X	X	X	X				
contrast	2	•	(31)	35	X	X				
arm style	(13)	22	•	X	X	X	X	X	X	
form	•	X	X	X	X	X				
midline	X	•	X	(27)	X	(28)	X	X		
x height	X	•	X	X						

ABCDEFG
HIJKLMN
OPQRSTU
VWXYZ
abcdefghijk
lmnopqrstu
vwxyz
123456789
0.,;:''&!?$

Times Roman 46 point

ABCDEFGHIJKLMN
OPQRSTUVWXYZ
abcdefghijklmnopqrstu
vwxyz
1234567890.,;:''&!?$

Times Italic 24 point

PANOSE abegmoqst

Times Semi Bold 24 point

PANOSE *abegmoqst*

Times Semi Bold Italic 24 point

PANOSE **abegmoqst**

Times Bold 24 point

PANOSE *abegmoqst*

Times Bold Italic 24 point

PANOSE **abegmoqst**

Times Extra Bold 24 point

Supplier	Linotronic 202 Digital Typesetter
Usage	Text, Display
Similar Fonts	Times Europa
Available Media	
Digital, DT, Photo, Hot, Bit, PS	
Alternate Names	
Dutch 801(BS), English(Alpha), English Times(CG), London Roman(Wang), Pegasus Press Roman(IBM), TR(Itek), Times New Roman(BH)	

	1	2	3	4	5	6	7	8	9	0
serif	●	68	93	X	X	X	(168)	X	(219)	X
proportion	●	(39)	X	X	X	X				
contrast	2	●	(31)	35	X	X				
arm style	(13)	22	●	X	X	X	X	X	X	
form	●	X	X	X	X	X				
midline	X	●	X	(27)	X	(28)	X	X		
x height	X	●	X	X						

ABCDEF
GHIJKLM
NOPQRS
TUVWXYZ
abcdefghijk
lmnopqrstu
vwxyz
123456789
0.,;:''&!?$

Cochin 44 point

ABCDEFGHIJKLMNO
PQRSTUVWXYZ
abcdefghijklmnopqrstuvw
xyz
1234567890.,;:''&!?$

Cochin Italic 24 point

PANOSE abegmoqst

Cochin Bold 24 point

PANOSE abegmoqst

Cochin Bold Italic 24 point

PANOSE abegmoqst

Cochin Black 24 point

PANOSE abegmoqst

Cochin Black Italic 24 point

Supplier	**Linotype 202 Digital Typesetter**
Usage	**Text, Display**
Similar Fonts	
Available Media	
Hot, Photo, Digital	
Alternate Names	
Le Cochin(BH)	

	1	2	3	4	5	6	7	8	9	0
serif	•	68	93	X	X	X	168	X	219	X
proportion	•	39	X	X	X	X				
contrast	3	•	31	35	X	X				
arm style	15	(22)	•	X	X	X	X	X	X	
form	•	X	X	X	X	X				
midline	X	X	•	X	X	X	X	X		
x height	•	X	X	X						

ABCDEFG HIJKLMN OPQRSTU VWXYZ abcdefghijkl mnopqrstuv wxyz 1234567 890.,;'"&!?$

Brighton Medium 48 point

ABCDEFGHIJKLMNOP QRSTUVWXYZ abcdefg hijklmnopqrstuvwxyz 1234567890.,;'"&!?$

Brighton Light 24 point

ABCDEFGHIJKLMNOP QRSTUVWXYZ abcdefg hijklmnopqrstuvwxyz 1234567890.,;'"&!?$

Brighton Light Italic 24 point

PANOSE abegmoqst

Brighton Bold 24 point

Supplier	**Alphatype CRS Digital Typesetter**
Usage	**Display, Text**
Similar Fonts	**Cooper 75**
Available Media	
Photo, Digital, DT	
Alternate Names	

	1	2	3	4	5	6	7	8	9	0
serif	•	68	93	X	X	X	168	X	219	X
proportion	•	39	X	X	X	X				
contrast	2	•	31	35	X	X				
arm style	(17)	22	•	X	X	X	X	X	X	
form	•	X	X	X	X	X				
midline	X	(23)	X	•	X	(28)	X	X		
x height	X	•	X	X						

ABCDEFGHIJ KLMNOP QRSTUVWX YZ
abcdefghijklm nopqr stuvwxyz 1234567890. ,;:''&!?$

Perpetua Roman 42 point

ABCDEFGHIJKLMNOPQR STUVWXYZ abcdefghijklmnopqrstuvw xyz 1234567890.,;:''&!?$

Perpetua Italic 24 point

ABCDEFGHIJKLMNO PQRSTUVWXYZ abcdefghijklmnopqrs tuvwxyz 1234567890.,;:''&!?$

Perpetua Bold 24 point

PANOSE abegmoqst

Perpetua Bold Italic 24 point

PANOSE abegmoqst

Perpetua Extra Bold 24 point

Supplier	**Compugraphic 8400 Digital Typesetter**
Usage	**Text, Display**
Similar Fonts	
Available Media	
Digital, DT, Photo, Hot, Bit	
Alternate Names	
Percepta(Alpha), Perpetual(Wang), Lapidary 333(BS)	

	1	2	3	4	5	6	7	8	9	0
serif	●	68	93	X	X	X	168	X	219	X
proportion	●	39	X	X	X	X				
contrast	2	●	31	35	X	X				
arm style	4	22	●	X	X	X	X	X	X	
form	●	X	X	X	X	X				
midline	X	23	X	27	X	●	X	X		
x height	X	●	X	X						

ABCDEFG
HIJKLMN
OPQRSTU
VWXYZ
abcdefghijkl
mnopqrstuv
wxyz
1234567
890.,;''&!?$

ITC Galliard 48 point

PANOSE abegmoqst

ITC Galliard Italic 24 point

PANOSE abegmoqst

ITC Galliard Bold 24 point

PANOSE abegmoqst

ITC Galliard Bold Italic 24 point

PANOSE abegmoqst

ITC Galliard Black 24 point

PANOSE abegmoqst

ITC Galliard Black Italic 24 point

PANOSE abegmoqst

ITC Galliard Ultra 24 point

PANOSE abegmoqst

ITC Galliard Ultra Italic 24 point

Supplier	**Alphatype CRS Digital Typesetter**
Usage	**Text, Display**
Similar Fonts	**Graphic Bold**
Available Media	
Photo, Digital, DT, Bit, PS	
Alternate Names	
Aldine 701(BS)	

	1	2	3	4	5	6	7	8	9	0
serif	•	X	X	X	X	X	X	X	X	X
proportion	•	40	54	X	61	X				
contrast	X	5	•	X	X	X				
arm style	•	X	31	X	X	X	X	X	X	
form	•	X	X	X	X	X				
midline	•	X	X	X	X	X	X	X		
x height	X	•	X	X						

ABCDEFG
HIJKLMNO
PQRSTUV
WXYZ abc
defghijklm
nopqrstuv
wxyz 1234
567890
.,;"&!?$

ITC Garamond Book 48 point

PANOSE abegmoqst

ITC Garamond Light 24 point

PANOSE abegmoqst

ITC Garamond Light Italic 24 point

PANOSE abegmoqst

ITC Garamond Book Italic 24 point

PANOSE abegmoqst

ITC Garamond Bold 24 point

PANOSE abegmoqst

ITC Garamond Bold Italic 24 point

PANOSE abegmoq

ITC Garamond Ultra 24 point

PANOSE abegmoq

ITC Garamond Ultra Italic 24 point

Supplier	**Alphatype CRS Digital Typesetter**
Usage	**Text, Display**
Similar Fonts	**Garamondus, Garamond No. 3**
Available Media	
Digital, DT, Photo, Hot, PS, Ludlow, Bit	
Alternate Names	
Aldine 851(BS), GD(Itek), Grenada(Wang), Garamont, Garamond(CG)	

	1	2	3	4	5	6	7	8	9	0
serif	●	X	X	X	X	X	X	X	X	X
proportion	●	40	54	X	61	X				
contrast	X	9	●	X	X	X				
arm style	●	X	31	X	X	X	X	X	X	
form	●	X	X	X	X	X				
midline	X	●	X	X	X	X	X	X		
x height	X	X	●	X						

ABCDEFG HIJKLMN OPQRSTU VWXYZ ab cdefghijklmn opqrstuvwxy 1234567890 .,;' '&!?$

Baskerville 48 point

ABCDEFGHIJKLMNO PQRSTUVWXYZ abcdefghijklmnopqrstu vwxyz 1234567890.,;:'&!?$

Baskerville Italic 24 point

ABCDEFGHIJKLMN OPQRSTUVWXYZ abcdefghijklmnopqrst uvwxyz 1234567890.,;:'&!?$

Baskerville Bold 24 point

PANOSE abegmoqst

Baskerville Bold Italic 24 point

Supplier	Alphatype CRS Digital Typesetter	
Usage	Text, Display	
Similar Fonts	Baskerville No.2, Baskerville 353	
Available Media		
Digital, Photo, Hot, DT, Bit		
Alternate Names		
Transitional 401(BS), BK(Itek), Baskerville II(CG), Beaumont(Wang)		

	1	2	3	4	5	6	7	8	9	0
serif	•	X	95	131	X	161	X	X	X	X
proportion	•	44	56	X	X	X				
contrast	2	23	•	35	X	X				
arm style	30	X	•	X	X	X	X	X	X	
form	•	X	X	X	X	X				
midline	X	•	X	X	X	X	X	X		
x height	X	•	X	X						

ABCDEFG
HIJKLMN
OPQRST
UVWXYZ
abcdefghij
klmnopqrs
tuvwxyz 1
234567890
.,;'"&!?$

ITC New Baskerville Semi-Bold 48 point

PANOSE abegmoqst

ITC New Baskerville 24 point

PANOSE abegmoqst

ITC New Baskerville Italic 24 point

PANOSE abegmoqst

ITC New Baskerville Semi-Bold Italic 24 point

PANOSE abegmoqst

ITC New Baskerville Bold 24 point

PANOSE abegmoqst

ITC New Baskerville Bold Italic 24 point

PANOSE abegmoqst

ITC New Baskerville Black 24 point

PANOSE abegmoqst

ITC New Baskerville Black Italic 24 point

Supplier	Alphatype CRS Digital Typesetter
Usage	Text, Display
Similar Fonts	Baker Danmark
Available Media	
Photo, Digital, PS, Bit	
Alternate Names	
Transitional 401(BS), BK(Itek), Beaumont(Wang)	

	1	2	3	4	5	6	7	8	9	0
serif	•	X	95	131	X	161	X	X	X	X
proportion	•	44	56	X	X	X				
contrast	2	23	•	35	X	X				
arm style	30	X	•	X	X	X	X	X	X	
form	•	X	X	X	X	X				
midline	X	•	X	X	X	X	X	X		
x height	X	•	X	X						

ABCDEF GHIJKLM NOPQRST UVWXYZ abcdefghijk lmnopqrstu vwxyz 123456789 0.,;:''&!?$

New Caledonia 48 point

PANOSE abegmoqst

New Caledonia Italic 24 point

PANOSE abegmoqst

New Caledonia Semi Bold Italic 24 point

PANOSE abegmoqst

New Caledonia Semi Bold 24 point

PANOSE abegmoqst

New Caledonia Bold 24 point

PANOSE abegmoqst

New Caledonia Bold Italic 24 point

PANOSE abegmoqst

New Caledonia Black 24 point

PANOSE abegmoqst

New Caledonia Black Italic 24 point

Supplier	Linotype 202 Digital Typesetter
Usage	Text, Display
Similar Fonts	
Available Media	
Photo, Digital	
Alternate Names	

Transitional 511(BS), Gemini, California(CG), Caledo(Alpha), Cornelia, Edinburg(Wang), Gale(III), Highland(Auto, Dymo), Laurel(HC)

	1	2	3	4	5	6	7	8	9	0
serif	•	X	95	131	X	161	X	X	X	X
proportion	•	44	56	X	X	X				
contrast	2	23	•	35	X	X				
arm style	30	X	•	X	X	X	X	X	X	
form	•	X	X	X	X	X				
midline	X	•	X	X	X	X	X	X		
x height	X	•	X	X						

ABCDEFGH
IJKLMNOP
QRSTUVW
XYZ
abcdefghijklm
nopqr
stuvwxyz
1234567890.
,;:''&!?$

Janson 42 point

ABCDEFGHIJKLMNO
PQRSTUVWXYZ
abcdefghijklmnopqrstuvw
xyz
1234567890.,;:''&!?$

Janson Italic 24 point

ABCDEFGHIJKLMN
OPQRSTUVWXYZ
abcdefghijklmnopqrstu
vwxyz
1234567890.,;:''&!?$

Janson Bold 24 point

PANOSE abegmoqst

Janson Bold Italic 24 point

Supplier	**Compugraphic 8400 Digital Typesetter**
Usage	**Text**
Similar Fonts	**Jason, Jenson**
Available Media	
Hot, Photo, Digital, Bit	
Alternate Names	
Dutch 721(BS)	

	1	2	3	4	5	6	7	8	9	0
serif	•	X	(95)	(131)	X	(161)	X	X	X	X
proportion	•	(44)	56	X	X	X				
contrast	2	(23)	•	35	X	X				
arm style	30	X	•	X	X	X	X	X	X	
form	•	X	X	X	X	X				
midline	X	•	X	X	X	X	X	X		
x height	X	•	X	X						

ABCDEFGHIJ
KLMNOP
QRSTUVWX
YZ
abcdefghijklmn
opqr
stuvwxyz
1234567890.,;
:"&!?$

Caslon No. 540 36 point

*ABCDEFGHIJ
KLMNOPQRST
UVWXYZ
abcdefghijklmno
pqrstuvwxyz
1234567890.,:.'
'&!?$*

Caslon No. 540 Italic 36 point

Supplier	**Compugraphic 8400 Digital Typesetter**
Usage	**Text, Display**
Similar Fonts	**Caslon, Caslon Old Face No.2**
Available Media	
Digital, DT, Photo, Hot, Bit	
Alternate Names	
Dutch 771(BS)	

	1	2	3	4	5	6	7	8	9	0
serif	●	X	X	X	X	X	X	X	X	X
proportion	●	X	57	X	X	X				
contrast	2	23	31	●	X	X				
arm style	X	X	●	X	X	X	X	X	X	
form	●	X	X	X	X	X				
midline	●	X	X	X	X	X	X	X		
x height	X	●	X	X						

ABCDEFG
HIJKLMN
OPQRSTU
VWXYZ
abcdefghij
klmnopqrs
tuvwxyz
1234567
890.,;"&!?

ITC Caslon No. 224 Regular 48 point

PANOSE abegmoqst

ITC Caslon No. 224 Light 24 point

PANOSE abegmoqst

ITC Caslon No. 224 Light Italic 24 point

PANOSE abegmoqst

ITC Caslon No. 224 Regular Italic 24 point

PANOSE abegmoqst

ITC Caslon No. 224 Bold 24 point

PANOSE abegmoqst

ITC Caslon No. 224 Bold Italic 24 point

PANOSE abegmoqst

ITC Caslon No. 224 Black 24 point

PANOSE abegmoqst

ITC Caslon No. 224 Black Italic 24 point

Supplier	Alphatype CRS Digital Typesetter
Usage	Text, Display
Similar Fonts	Classic
Available Media	
Photo, Digital, Bit	
Alternate Names	
LSC Caslon 223(CG), Dutch 761(BS), Dutch 776(BS)	

	1	2	3	4	5	6	7	8	9	0
serif	●	X	X	X	X	X	X	X	X	X
proportion	●	X	X	X	64	X				
contrast	X	X	X	X	●	X				
arm style	X	X	X	X	●	X	X	X	X	
form	●.	X	X	X	X	X				
midline	●	X	X	X	X	X	X	X		
x height	X	X	X	X						

Camelot

ABCDEFGHI
JKLMNOP
QRSTUVW
XYZ
abcdefghijkl
mnopqr
stuvwxyz
1234567890.,;
:'&!?$

Camelot 48 point

ABCDEFGHIJKLMNOPQR STUVWXYZ abcdefghij klmnopqrstuvwxyz 1234567890.,;:''&!?$

Camelot Italic 24 point

ABCDEFGHIJKLMN OPQRSTUVWXYZ abcdefghijklmnopqrs tuvwxyz 1234567890.,;:''&!?$

Camelot Bold 24 point

PANOSE abegmoqst

Camelot Extrabold 24 point

PANOSE abegmoqst

Camelot Black 24 point

Supplier	Compugraphic 8400 Digital Typesetter
Usage	Display
Similar Fonts	
Available Media	
Photo, Digital	
Alternate Names	

	1	2	3	4	5	6	7	8	9	0
serif	●	X	X	X	X	X	170	212	X	236
proportion	●	X	X	X	X	X				
contrast	X	X	X	X	X	●				
arm style	X	X	X	●	X	X	X	X	X	
form	X	●	X	X	X	X				
midline	X	X	X	●	X	X	X	X		
x height	X	●	X	X						

ABCDEFG
HIJKLMNO
PQRSTUV
WXYZ abc
defghijklm
nopqrstuv
wxyz 1234
567890.,;""
&!?$

Caxton Book 48 point

PANOSE abegmoqst

Caxton Light 24 point

PANOSE abegmoqst

Caxton Light Italic 24 point

PANOSE abegmoqst

Caxton Book Italic 24 point

PANOSE abegmoqst

Caxton Bold 24 point

PANOSE abegmoqst

Caxton Bold Italic 24 point

PANOSE abegmoqst

Caxton Roman Bold Condensed 24 point

PANOSE abegmoqst

Caxton Extra Bold 24 point

PANOSE abegmoqst

Caxton Extra Bold Italic 24 point

Supplier	Alphatype CRS Digital Typesetter
Usage	Display, Text
Similar Fonts	
Available Media	
Photo, Digital, DT	
Alternate Names	

	1	2	3	4	5	6	7	8	9	0
serif	•	71	X	X	150	X	X	X	X	X
proportion	16	•	53	X	60	X				
contrast	X	•	40	X	X	X				
arm style	•	X	39	X	X	X	X	X	X	
form	•	X	X	X	X	X				
midline	X	X	•	X	X	X	X	X		
x height	X	X	•	X						

ABCDEF
GHIJKLM
NOPQRS
TUVWXY
Z
abcdefghij
klmnopqr
stuvwxyz
12345678
90.,;:''&!?$

Primer 54 Semi-Bold 48 point

PANOSEabegmoqst

Primer 54 24 point

PANOSEabegmoqst

Primer 54 Italic 24 point

PANOSEabegmoqst

Primer 54 Semi-Bold Italic 24 point

PANOSEabegmoqst

Primer 54 Bold 24 point

PANOSEabegmoqst

Primer 54 Bold Italic 24 point

PANOSEabegmoqst

Primer 54 Black 24 point

PANOSEabegmoqst

Primer 54 Black Italic 24 point

Supplier	Linotronic 300 Laser Typesetter
Usage	Text, Display
Similar Fonts	Stratford
Available Media	
Photo, Digital, Hot	
Alternate Names	
Rector(Alpha), Primer	

	1	2	3	4	5	6	7	8	9	0
serif	•	72	103	134	X	163	X	X	224	X
proportion	23	•	X	X	X	X				
contrast	X	•	44	X	X	X				
arm style	38	X	•	X	X	X	X	X	X	
form	•	X	X	X	X	X				
midline	X	•	X	X	X	X	X	X		
x height	X	•	X	X						

ABCDEF
GHIJKLM
NOPQRST
UVWXYZ
abcdefghij
klmnopqrs
tuvwxyz
12345678
90.,;:''&!?$

Leamington Medium 42 point

ABCDEFGHIJKLMN
OPQRSTUVWXYZ
abcdefghijklmnopqrst
uvwxyz
1234567890.,;:''&!?$

Leamington 23 point

*ABCDEFGHIJKLMN
OPQRSTUVWXYZ
abcdefghijklmnopqrstu
vwxyz
1234567890.,;:''&!?$*

Leamington Italic 23 point

PANOSE abegmoqs

Leamington Bold 24 point

PANOSE abegmoq

Leamington Black 24 point

Supplier	Linotronic 202 Digital Typesetter
Usage	Text, Display
Similar Fonts	Allgentine
Available Media	
Photo, Digital	
Alternate Names	

	1	2	3	4	5	6	7	8	9	0
serif	●	X	105	X	151	X	X	X	X	X
proportion	29	●	54	X	61	X				
contrast	X	38	●	X	X	X				
arm style	●	X	41	X	45	X	X	X	X	
form	●	X	X	X	X	X				
midline	●	X	X	X	X	X	X	X		
x height	X	●	X	X						

ABCDEF GHIJKLM NOPQRS TUVWXY abcdefghij klmnopqr stuvwxyz 1234567 890.,;''&!?

ITC Esprit 48 point

PANOSE abegmoqst

ITC Esprit Book 24 point

PANOSE abegmoqst

ITC Esprit Book Italic 24 point

PANOSE abegmoqst

ITC Esprit Medium Italic 24 point

PANOSE abegmoqst

ITC Esprit Bold 24 point

PANOSE abegmoqst

ITC Esprit Bold Italic 24 point

PANOSE abegmoqst

ITC Esprit Black 24 point

PANOSE abegmoqst

ITC Esprit Black Italic 24 point

Supplier	Alphatype CRS Digital Typesetter
Usage	Display, Text
Similar Fonts	
Available Media	
Photo, Digital	
Alternate Names	

	1	2	3	4	5	6	7	8	9	0
serif	•	74	106	135	X	164	X	X	X	X
proportion	31	•	56	X	X	X				
contrast	X	39	•	X	X	X				
arm style	40	X	•	X	45	X	X	X	X	
form	•	X	X	X	X	X				
midline	•	44	X	X	X	X	X	X		
x height	X	•	43	X						

ABCDEF
GHIJKLM
NOPQRST
UVWXYZ
abcdefghij
klmnopqr
stuvwxyz
123456789
0.,;:"&!?$

New Aster Semi-Bold 48 point

PANOSE abegmoqst

New Aster 24 point

PANOSE *abegmoqst*

New Aster Italic 24 point

PANOSE *abegmoqst*

New Aster Semi-Bold Italic 24 point

PANOSE abegmoqst

New Aster Bold 24 point

PANOSE *abegmoqst*

New Aster Bold Italic 24 point

PANOSE abegmoqst

New Aster Black 24 point

PANOSE *abegmoqst*

New Aster Black Italic 24 point

Supplier	**Linotronic 300 Laser Typesetter**
Usage	**Text, Display**
Similar Fonts	**Aster, Horizon**
Available Media	
Photo, Digital	
Alternate Names	

	1	2	3	4	5	6	7	8	9	0
serif	•	74	106	135	X	164	X	X	X	X
proportion	31	•	56	X	X	X				
contrast	X	39	•	X	X	X				
arm style	40	X	•	X	45	X	X	X	X	
form	•	X	X	X	X	X				
midline	•	44	X	X	X	X	X	X		
x height	X	•	43	X						

ABCDEF
GHIJKLM
NOPQRS
TUVWXYZ
abcdefghij
klmnopqrs
tuvwxyz
12345678
90.,;:"&!?$

Romana Normal 46 point

ABCDEFGHIJKLMN
OPQRSTUVWXYZ
abcdefghijklmnopqr
stuvwxyz
1234567890.,;:"&!?$

Romana Bold 24 point

ABCDEFGHIJKLMN
OPQRSTUVWXYZ
abcdefghijklmnopqr
stuvwxyz
1234567890.,;:"&!?$

Romana Extra Bold 24 point

Supplier	Linotronic 202 Digital Typesetter
Usage	Display, Text
Similar Fonts	Largo
Available Media	
Photo, Digital	
Alternate Names	

	1	2	3	4	5	6	7	8	9	0
serif	•	74	**108**	135	X	164	X	X	X	X
proportion	31	•	56	X	X	X				
contrast	X	39	•	X	X	X				
arm style	40	X	•	X	45	X	X	X	X	
form	•	X	X	X	X	X				
midline	•	X	X	X	X	X	X	X		
x height	X	41	•	X						

ABCDEFG HIJKLMN OPQRSTU VWXYZ abcdefghij klmnopqrs tuvwxyz 123456789 0.,;:''&!?$

Gazette 40 point

ABCDEFGHIJKLMN OPQRSTUVWXYZ abcdefghijklmnopqrs tuvwxyz 1234567890.,;:''&!?$

Gazette Italic 22 point

ABCDEFGHIJKLM NOPQRSTUVWXYZ abcdefghijklmnopqr stuvwxyz 1234567890.,;:''&!?$

Gazette Bold 22 point

Supplier	**Linotype 202 Digital Typesetter**
Usage	**Text, Display**
Similar Fonts	
Available Media	
Photo, Digital, Bit	
Alternate Names	
Dutch 802(BS), Imperial(HC), News No.4(CG), Bedford(Auto, Dymo), New Bedford(Auto), Newstext, Taurus	

	1	2	3	4	5	6	7	8	9	0
serif	•	74	(109)	135	X	(164)	X	X	X	X
proportion	(31)	•	56	X	X	X				
contrast	X	(39)	•	X	X	X				
arm style	40	X	•	X	(46)	X	X	X	X	
form	•	X	X	X	X	X				
midline	(41)	•	X	X	X	X	X	X		
x height	X	•	X	X						

ABCDEFG
HIJKLMN
OPQRSTU
VWXYZ
abcdefghijkl
mnopqrstuv
wxyz
1234567890
.,;:'"&!?$

ABCDEFGHIJKLM
NOPQRSTUVWXYZ
abcdefghijklmnopqrst
uvwxyz
1234567890.,;:'"&!?$

ABCDEFGHIJKLM
NOPQRSTUVWXYZ
abcdefghijklmnopq
rstuvwxyz
1234567890.,;:'"&!?$

Supplier	Linotronic 202 Digital Typesetter
Usage	**Text**
Similar Fonts	**Period Old Style**
Available Media	
Photo, Digital, Bit	
Alternate Names	
Dutch 766(BS)	

	1	2	3	4	5	6	7	8	9	0
serif	•	75	110	X	X	X	X	X	X	X
proportion	X	•	X	X	62	X				
contrast	X	X	•	(48)	X	X				
arm style	(40)	X	(41)	X	•	X	X	X	X	
form	•	X	X	X	X	X				
midline	•	(46)	X	X	X	X	X	X		
x height	X	•	X	X						

ABCDEF
GHIJKLM
NOPQRST
UVWXYZ
abcdefghij
klmnopqrs
tuvwxyz
1234567
890.,;''&!?$

ITC Century Book 48 point

PANOSE abegmoqst

ITC Century Light 24 point

PANOSE abegmoqst

ITC Century Light Italic 24 point

PANOSE abegmoqst

ITC Century Book Italic 24 point

PANOSE abegmoq

ITC Century Bold 24 point

PANOSE abegmoq

ITC Century Bold Italic 24 point

PANOSE abegm

ITC Century Ultra 24 point

PANOSE abegm

ITC Century Ultra Italic 24 point

Supplier	**Alphatype CRS Digital Typesetter**
Usage	**Text, Display**
Similar Fonts	
Available Media	
Digital, Hot, Photo, Bit	
Alternate Names	

Century 711(BS), Cambridge Expanded(Wang), CE(Itek), Century Expanded(Alpha, AM, Auto, Dymo, HC, Merg), Century Light(CG)

	1	2	3	4	5	6	7	8	9	0
serif	•	75	(110)	X	X	X	X	X	X	X
proportion	X	•	X	X	62	X				
contrast	X	X	•	51	X	X				
arm style	40	X	(44)	X	•	X	X	X	X	
form	•	X	X	X	X	X				
midline	(45)	•	X	X	X	X	X	X		
x height	X	•	47	X						

ABCDEFG
HIJKLMN
OPQRSTU
VWXYZ
abcdefghij
klmnopqr
stuvwxyz
1234567
890.,;"&!?

ITC Isbell Medium 48 point

PANOSE abegmoqst

ITC Isbell Book 24 point

PANOSE abegmoqst

ITC Isbell Book Italic 24 point

PANOSE abegmoqst

ITC Isbell Medium Italic 24 point

PANOSE abegmoqst

ITC Isbell Bold 24 point

PANOSE abegmoqst

ITC Isbell Bold Italic 24 point

PANOSE abegmoq

ITC Isbell Heavy 24 point

PANOSE abegmoq

ITC Isbell Heavy Italic 24 point

Supplier	Alphatype CRS Digital Typesetter
Usage	Display, Text
Similar Fonts	
Available Media	
Photo, Digital, Bit, DT	
Alternate Names	
Revival 821(BS)	

	1	2	3	4	5	6	7	8	9	0
serif	•	75	112	X	X	X	X	X	X	X
proportion	X	•	X	X	62	X				
contrast	X	X	•	51	X	X				
arm style	40	X	44	X	•	X	X	X	X	
form	•	X	X	X	X	X				
midline	X	•	X	X	X	X	X	X		
x height	X	46	•	X						

ABCDEFG HIJKLMN OPQRSTU VWXYZ

abcdefghijk lmnopqrst uvwxyz 123456789 0.,;:"&!?$

Madison Medium 44 point

ABCDEFGHIJKLMNO PQRSTUVWXYZ abcdefghijklmnopqrstu vwxyz 1234567890.,;:"&!?$

Madison Bold 17 point

ABCDEFGHIJKLMNO PQRSTUVWXYZ abcdefghijklmnopqrstu vwxyz 1234567890.,;:"&!?$

Madison Medium Condensed 24 point

PANOSE abegmoqst

Madison 24 point

PANOSE abegmoqst

Madison Italic 24 point

Supplier	Linotronic 300 Laser Typesetter
Usage	Display, Text
Similar Fonts	Graphis
Available Media	
Photo, Digital	
Alternate Names	

	1	2	3	4	5	6	7	8	9	0
serif	•	X	X	137	X	X	178	X	X	X
proportion	X	•	59	X	63	X				
contrast	X	X	(45)	•	X	X				
arm style	X	X	X	X	•	X	X	X	X	
form	•	X	X	X	X	X				
midline	•	(51)	X	X	X	X	X	X		
x height	X	•	(50)	X						

ABCDEF GHIJKL MNOPQR STUVWX abcdefghi jklmnopq rstuvwxy 1234567890.,;&

ITC Tiffany Medium 48 point

PANOSE abegmoqst

ITC Tiffany Light 24 point

PANOSE abegmoqst

ITC Tiffany Light Italic 24 point

PANOSE abegmoqst

ITC Tiffany Medium Italic 24 point

PANOSE abegmoq

ITC Tiffany Demi 24 point

PANOSE abegmoqs

ITC Tiffany Demi Italic 24 point

PANOSE abegmo

ITC Tiffany Heavy 24 point

PANOSE abegm

ITC Tiffany Heavy Italic 24 point

Supplier	Alphatype CRS Digital Typesetter
Usage	Display
Similar Fonts	Grouch
Available Media	
Digital, Photo, DT, Bit, PS	
Alternate Names	
Revival 831(BS)	

	1	2	3	4	5	6	7	8	9	0
serif	•	X	X	137	X	X	178	X	X	X
proportion	X	•	59	X	63	X				
contrast	X	X	(45)	•	X	X				
arm style	X	X	X	X	•	X	X	X	X	
form	•	X	X	X	X	X				
midline	•	(51)	X	X	X	X	X	X		
x height	X	•	(50)	X						

ABCDEFG
HIJKLMN
OPQRSTU
VWXYZ
abcdefghij
klmnopqr
stuvwxyz
1234567
890.,;"&!?$

ITC Modern No. 216 Medium 48 point

PANOSE abegmoqst

ITC Modern No. 216 24 point

PANOSE abegmoqst

ITC Modern No. 216 Italic 24 point

PANOSE abegmoqst

ITC Modern No. 216 Medium Italic 24 point

PANOSE abegmoqst

ITC Modern No. 216 Bold 24 point

PANOSE abegmoqst

ITC Modern No. 216 Bold Italic 24 point

PANOSE abegmoq

ITC Modern No. 216 Heavy 24 point

PANOSE abegmoq

ITC Modern No. 216 Heavy Italic 24 point

Supplier	**Alphatype CRS Digital Typesetter**
Usage	**Display, Text**
Similar Fonts	**De Vinne, Highland**
Available Media	
Photo, Digital	
Alternate Names	

	1	2	3	4	5	6	7	8	9	0
serif	•	X	X	137	X	X	(178)	X	X	X
proportion	X	•	59	X	63	X				
contrast	X	X	45	•	X	X				
arm style	X	X	X	X	•	X	X	X	X	
form	•	X	X	X	X	X				
midline	•	X	X	X	X	X	X	X		
x height	X	(48)	•	X						

ABCDEFG HIJKLMN OPQRST UVWXYZ abcdefghijk lmnopqrstu vwxyz 123456789 0.,;:''&!?$

Bulmer 48 point

ABCDEFGHIJ KLMNOPORST UVWXYZ abcdefghijklmno pqrstuvwxyz 1234567890 .,;:''&!?$

Bulmer Italic 36 point

Supplier	**Linotype 202 Digital Typesetter**
Usage	**Text**
Similar Fonts	**Hawthorne**
Available Media	
Photo, Digital, Hot	
Alternate Names	

	1	2	3	4	5	6	7	8	9	0
serif	•	X	X	**137**	X	X	178	X	X	X
proportion	X	•	59	X	63	X				
contrast	X	X	46	•	X	X				
arm style	X	X	X	X	•	X	X	X	X	
form	•	X	X	X	X	X				
midline	48	•	X	X	X	X	X	X		
x height	X	•	X	X						

ABCDEFG HIJKLMN OPQRST UVWXYZ abcdefghijkl mnopqrstuv wxyz 12345 67890.,;"&!?

Cloister Old Style 48 point

ABCDEFGHIJKLMNOP QRSTUVWXYZ abcdefghijklmnopqrstuvwxyz 1234567890.,;"&!?$

Cloister Old Style Italic 24 point

ABCDEFGHIJKLMN OPQRSTUVWXYZ abcdefghijklmnopqrst uvwxyz 1234567890.,;"&!?$

Cloister Bold 24 point

PANOSE abegmoqst

Cloister Bold Italic 24 point

Supplier	Alphatype CRS Digital Typesetter
Usage	Text
Similar Fonts	Cooper Oldstyle, Cloister
Available Media	
Hot, Photo, Digital, DT,	
Alternate Names	
Eusebius(Ludlow), Nicholas Jenson, CG Cloister(CG), Cloister(Merg)	

	1	2	3	4	5	6	7	8	9	0
serif	•	78	X	X	152	X	X	X	X	X
proportion	X	X	•	X	X	X				
contrast	•	53	54	X	X	X				
arm style	•	X	X	X	X	X	X	X	X	
form	•	X	X	X	X	X				
midline	X	•	X	X	X	X	X	X		
x height	•	X	X	X						

ABCDEFG
HIJKLMN
OPQRSTU
VWXYZ
abcdefghij
klmnopqrs
tuvwxyz
1234567
890.,;"&!?$

ITC Novarese Medium 48 point

ABCDEFGHIJKLMNO
PQRSTUVWXYZ
*abcdefghijklmnopq
rstuvwxyz*
1234567890.,;"&!?$

ITC Novarese Medium Italic 24 point

PANOSE abegmoqst

ITC Novarese Book 24 point

PANOSE *abegmoqst*

ITC Novarese Book Italic 24 point

PANOSE abegmoqst

ITC Novarese Bold 24 point

PANOSE *abegmoqst*

ITC Novarese Bold Italic 24 point

PANOSE abegmoq

ITC Novarese Ultra 24 point

Supplier	**Alphatype CRS Digital Typesetter**
Usage	**Display, Text**
Similar Fonts	**Bernase, Keene Condensed**
Available Media	
Photo, Digital, DT	
Alternate Names	

	1	2	3	4	5	6	7	8	9	0
serif	•	X	X	142	X	X	X	X	X	X
proportion	5	38	•	X	60	X				
contrast	52	•	54	X	X	X				
arm style	•	X	X	X	X	X	X	X	X	
form	•	X	X	X	X	X				
midline	•	X	X	X	X	X	X	X		
x height	X	•	X	X						

ABCDEF GHIJKLM NOPQRST UVWXYZ abcdefghij klmnopqrs tuvwxyz 12345678 90.,;"&!?$

Adroit Medium 48 point

ABCDEFGHIJKLM NOPQRSTUVWXYZ abcdefghijklmnopq rstuvwxyz 1234567890.,;"&!?$

Adroit Medium Italic 24 point

PANOSE abegmoqst

Adroit Light 24 point

PANOSE abegmoqst

Adroit Light Italic 24 point

PANOSE abegmoqs

Adroit Bold 24 point

PANOSE abegmoqst

Adroit Black 24 point

Supplier	**Alphatype CRS Digital Typesetter**
Usage	**Text, Display**
Similar Fonts	
Available Media	
Photo, Digital	
Alternate Names	

	1	2	3	4	5	6	7	8	9	0
serif	•	X	X	X	(156)	X	X	X	X	X
proportion	29	40	•	X	61	X				
contrast	52	53	•	X	X	X				
arm style	•	55	56	X	X	X	X	X	X	
form	•	X	X	X	X	X				
midline	•	X	X	X	X	X	X	X		
x height	X	X	•	X						

ABCDEFGH IJKLMNOP QRSTUVW XYZ
abcdefghijkl
mnopqr
stuvwxyz
123456789
0.,;:''&!?$

Windsor Old Style Light 42 point

ABCDEFGHIJKLMNOPQ
RSTUVWXYZ
abcdefghijklmnopqrstuvwx
yz
1234567890.,;:''&!?$

Windsor Light Condensed 24 point

**ABCDEFGHIJKLMN
OPQRSTUVWXYZ
abcdefghijklmnopqrs
tuvwxyz
1234567890.,;:''&!?$**

Windsor Bold 21 point

PANOSE abegmoqst

Windsor Elongated 24 point

PANOSE abegmoqst

Windsor Compact 24 point

Supplier	**Compugraphic 8400 Digital Typesetter**
Usage	**Display**
Similar Fonts	**Musketeer, Pabst**
Available Media	
Digital, DT, Photo, Hot, Bit	
Alternate Names	
Revival 801(BS), News 701, Winslow(Alpha)	

	1	2	3	4	5	6	7	8	9	0
serif	●	X	X	X	X	X	X	X	X	X
proportion	X	X	●	X	X	X				
contrast	X	X	●	X	X	X				
arm style	54	●	56	X	X	X	X	X	X	
form	X	X	X	X	●	X				
midline	X	X	●	X	X	X	X	X		
x height	X	●	X	X						

ABCDEFGH
IJKLMNOP
QRSTUVW
XYZ abcdef
ghijklmno
pqrstuvw
xyz 123456
7890.,;"'&!?

ITC Zapf International Medium 48 point

PANOSE abegmoqst

ITC Zapf International Light 24 point

PANOSE abegmoqst

ITC Zapf International Light Italic 24 point

PANOSE abegmoqst

ITC Zapf International Medium Italic 24 point

PANOSE abegmoqst

ITC Zapf International Demi 24 point

PANOSE abegmoqst

ITC Zapf International Demi Italic 24 point

PANOSE abegmoqst

ITC Zapf International Heavy 24 point

PANOSE abegmoqst

ITC Zapf International Heavy Italic 24 point

Supplier	**Alphatype CRS Digital Typesetter**
Usage	**Display, Text**
Similar Fonts	
Available Media	
Photo, Digital, Bit	
Alternate Names	
Elliptical 717(BS)	

	1	2	3	4	5	6	7	8	9	0
serif	•	X	X	(143)	X	167	X	X	X	X
proportion	31	41	•	X	X	X				
contrast	X	X	•	57	X	X				
arm style	54	55	•	X	X	X	X	X	X	
form	X	•	X	X	X	X				
midline	•	X	X	X	X	X	X	X		
x height	X	•	X	X						

ABCDEFG HIJKLMN OPQRSTU VWXYZ
abcdefghijk lmnopqrst uvwxyz
1234567890.,;:'"&!?$

Lucian 48 point

ABCDEFGHI JKLMNOPQ RSTUVWXYZ
abcdefghijklm nopqrstuvwxyz
1234567890.,; :'"&!?$

Lucian Bold 36 point

Supplier	**Linotronic 300 Laser Typesetter**
Usage	**Display, Text**
Similar Fonts	
Available Media	
Photo, Digital, Hot	
Alternate Names	

	1	2	3	4	5	6	7	8	9	0
serif	•	X	124	X	X	X	X	X	X	X
proportion	35	X	•	X	X	X				
contrast	X	X	56	•	X	X				
arm style	X	X	•	X	59	X	X	X	X	
form	•	X	X	X	X	X				
midline	X	•	X	X	X	X	X	X		
x height	•	X	X	X						

ABCDEFG HIJKLMN OPQRSTU VWXYZ abcdefghij klmnopqr stuvwxyz 1234567 890.,;"&!?$

Independence 36 point

ABCDEFGHIJKLM NOPQRSTUVWXY abcdefghijklmnopq rstuvwxyz 123456 7890.,;"&!?$

Independence Italic 24 point

ABCDEFGHIJKLM NOPQRSTUVWXY abcdefghijklmnop qrstuvwxyz 1234 567890.,;"&!?$

Independence Bold 24 point

PANOSE abegmo

Independence Extrabold 24 point

PANOSE abegmo

Independence Black 24 point

Supplier	Alphatype CRS Digital Typesetter
Usage	Display, Text
Similar Fonts	Concorde, Freedom
Available Media	
Photo, Digital, Hot, DT, Bit	
Alternate Names	
American Classic(CG), Colonial(AM), Americana(Merg), Flareserif 721(BS)	

	1	2	3	4	5	6	7	8	9	0
serif	•	X	124	X	X	X	X	X	X	X
proportion	35	X	•	X	X	X				
contrast	X	X	56	•	X	X				
arm style	X	X	•	X	59	X	X	X	X	
form	•	X	X	X	X	X				
midline	X	X	X	X	X	•	X	X		
x height	X	X	•	X						

ABCDEFGH
IJKLMNOP
QRSTUVWX
YZ
abcdefghijkl
mnopqr
stuvwxyz
1234567890.,;:
'&!?$

Devinne 36 point

ABCDEFGHI
JKLMNOPQR
STUVWXYZ
abcdefghijklm
nopqrstuvwxyz
1234567890.,;:"
&!?$

Devinne Italic 33 point

Supplier	**Compugraphic 8400 Digital Typesetter**
Usage	**Display, Text**
Similar Fonts	
Available Media	
Hot, Photo, Digital	
Alternate Names	

	1	2	3	4	5	6	7	8	9	0
serif	●	X	X	X	X	X	X	X	X	X
proportion	X	(51)	●	X	(63)	X				
contrast	X	X	X	●	X	X				
arm style	X	X	57	X	●	X	X	X	X	
form	●	X	X	X	X	X				
midline	X	●	X	X	X	X	X	X		
x height	X	●	X	X						

ABCDEFGHI JKLMNOPQR STUVWXYZ abcdefghijkl mnopqrstuv wxyz 12345 67890 .,;"&!?$

ITC Benguiat Condensed Medium 48 point

ABCDEFGHIJKLMNOPQR STUVWXYZ abcdefghijkl mnopqrstuvwxyz 1234567890.,;"&!?$

ITC Benguiat Condensed Medium Italic 24 point

PANOSE abegmoqst

ITC Benguiat Condensed Book 24 point

PANOSE abegmoqst

ITC Benguiat Condensed Book Italic 24 point

PANOSE abegmoqst

ITC Benguiat Condensed Bold 24 point

PANOSE abegmoqst

ITC Benguiat Condensed Bold Italic 24 point

Supplier	**Alphatype CRS Digital Typesetter**
Usage	**Display, Text**
Similar Fonts	**Caslon Condensed**
Available Media	
Photo, Digital	
Alternate Names	
Revival 832(BS)	

	1	2	3	4	5	6	7	8	9	0
serif	•	X	X	X	X	X	X	X	X	X
proportion	16	38	53	X	•	X				
contrast	X	•	61	X	X	X				
arm style	•	X	X	X	X	X	X	X	X	
form	•	X	X	X	X	X				
midline	X	X	•	X	X	X	X	X		
x height	X	X	•	X						

ABCDEFGHIJ
KLMNOP
QRSTUVWX
YZ
abcdefghijkl
mnopqr
stuvwxyz
1234567890
.,;:''&!?$

Garamond Medium Condensed 48 point

PANOSE abegmoqst

Garamond Light Condensed 24 point

PANOSE abegmoqst

Garamond Light Condensed Italic 24 point

PANOSE abegmoqst

Garamond Medium Condensed Italic 24 point

PANOSE abegmoqst

Garamond Bold Condensed 24 point

PANOSE abegmoqst

Garamond Bold Condensed Italic 24 point

PANOSE abegmoqst

Garamond Ultra Condensed 24 point

PANOSE abegmoqst

Garamond Ultra Condensed Italic 24 point

Supplier	Alphatype CRS Digital Typesetter
Usage	Display, Text
Similar Fonts	
Available Media	
Hot, Photo, Digital, DT, Bit	
Alternate Names	
Aldine 851(BS), GD(Itek), Grenada(Wang), Garamont, Garamond(CG)	

	1	2	3	4	5	6	7	8	9	0
serif	●	X	X	X	X	X	X	X	X	X
proportion	30	40	54	X	●	X				
contrast	X	60	●	X	X	X				
arm style	●	X	X	X	62	X	X	X	X	
form	●	X	X	X	X	X				
midline	X	●	X	X	X	X	X	X		
x height	X	X	●	X						

ABCDEFGH
IJKLMNOP
QRSTUVWX
YZ abcdefgh
ijklmnopqrs
tuvwxyz
1234567890
.,;"&!?$

ITC Century Book Condensed 48 point

PANOSE abegmoqst

ITC Century Light Condensed 24 point

PANOSE abegmoqst

ITC Century Light Condensed Italic 24 point

PANOSE abegmoqst

ITC Century Book Condensed Italic 24 point

PANOSE abegmoqst

ITC Century Bold Condensed 24 point

PANOSE abegmoqst

ITC Century Bold Condensed Italic 24 point

PANOSE abegmoqst

ITC Century Ultra Condensed 24 point

PANOSE abegmoqst

ITC Century Ultra Condensed Italic 24 point

Supplier	Alphatype CRS Digital Typesetter
Usage	Display, Text
Similar Fonts	
Available Media	
Hot, Photo, Digital, Bit	
Alternate Names	
Century 711(BS), Cambridge Expanded(Wang), CE(Itek), Century Expanded(Alpha, AM, Auto, Dymo, HC, Merg), Century Light(CG)	

	1	2	3	4	5	6	7	8	9	0
serif	•	X	X	X	X	X	X	X	X	X
proportion	X	46	X	X	•	X				
contrast	X	X	•	63	64	X				
arm style	61	X	X	X	•	X	X	X	X	
form	•	X	X	X	X	X				
midline	X	•	X	X	X	X	X	X		
x height	X	•	X	X						

ABCDEFG HIJKLMN OPQRSTUV WXYZ abcdefghijk lmnopqrstu vwxyz 123456789 0.,:;"&!?$

Century Nova 48 point

ABCDEFGHIJK LMNOPQRSTUV WXYZ abcdefghijklmnop qrstuvwxyz 1234567890.,:;"&! ?$

Century Nova Italic 36 point

Supplier	Linotype 300 Laser Typesetter
Usage	Display, Text
Similar Fonts	Onyx
Available Media	
Photo, Hot, Digital	
Alternate Names	

	1	2	3	4	5	6	7	8	9	0
serif	●	X	128	X	X	X	X	X	X	X
proportion	X	(51)	(59)	X	●	X				
contrast	X	X	(62)	●	(64)	X				
arm style	X	X	X	X	●	X	X	X	X	
form	●	X	X	X	X	X				
midline	X	●	X	X	X	X	X	X		
x height	X	●	X	X						

ABCDEF
GHIJKLM
NOPQRST
UVWXYZ
abcdefghij
klmnopqr
stuvwxyz
123456789
0.,;:"&!?$

Trooper 48 point

ABCDEFGHIJKLM
NOPQRSTUVWXYZ
abcdefghijklm
nopqrstuvwxyz
1234567890..,;:"&!?$

Trooper Italic. 24 point

PANOSE abegmoqst

Trooper Light 24 point

PANOSE abegmoqst

Trooper Light Italic 24 point

PANOSE abegmoqst

Trooper Bold 24 point

PANOSE abegmoqst

Trooper Extra Bold 24 point

PANOSE abegmoqst

Trooper Black 24 point

Supplier	Linotronic 202 Digital Typesetter
Usage	Display, Text
Similar Fonts	
Available Media	
Hot, Photo, Digital, DT	
Alternate Names	

	1	2	3	4	5	6	7	8	9	0
serif	•	X	X	X	X	X	X	X	X	X
proportion	36	X	X	X	•	X				
contrast	X	X	(62)	(63)	•	X				
arm style	X	X	X	X	•	X	X	X	X	
form	•	X	X	X	X	X				
midline	X	•	X	X	X	X	X	X		
x height	X	•	X	X						

ABCDEFG HIJKLMN OPQRSTU VWXYZ abcdefghij klmnopqr stuvwxyz 123456789 0.,;:''&!?$

Joanna 46 point

ABCDEFGHIJKLMNOP QRSTUVWXYZ abcdefghijklmnopqrst uvwxyz 1234567890.,;:''&!?$

Joanna Italic 24 point

ABCDEFGHIJKLM NOPQRSTUVWXYZ abcdefghijklmnop qrstuvwxyz 1234567890.,;:''&!?$

Joanna Bold 24 point

PANOSE abegmoqst

Joanna Extra Bold 24 point

Supplier	Linotronic 202 Digital Typesetter
Usage	Text, Display
Similar Fonts	
Available Media	
Photo, Digital	
Alternate Names	

	1	2	3	4	5	6	7	8	9	0
serif	2	●	89	X	X	X	X	X	X	X
proportion	●	X	X	X	X	X				
contrast	●	68	X	X	X	X				
arm style	X	X	●	X	X	X	X	X	X	
form	●	X	X	X	X	X				
midline	●	X	X	X	X	X	X	X		
x height	X	●	X	X						

ABCDEFG
HIJKLMN
OPQRSTU
VWXYZ
abcdefghijk
lmnopqrstu
vwxyz
123456789
0.,;:"&!?$

Breughel 55 42 point

ABCDEFGHIJKLM
NOPQRSTUVWXYZ
abcdefghijklmnopqrst
uvwxyz
1234567890.,;:"&!?$

Breughel 56 24 point

PANOSE abegmoqst

Breughel 65 24 point

PANOSE abegmoqst

Breughel 66 24 point

PANOSE abegmoqst

Breughel 75 24 point

PANOSE abegmoqst

Breughel 76 24 point

Supplier	Linotype 202 Digital Typesetter	
Usage	Text, Display	
Similar Fonts	Weiss	
Available Media		
Photo, Digital		
Alternate Names		

	1	2	3	4	5	6	7	8	9	0
serif	5	•	90	129	X	160	X	X	X	X
proportion	•	71	X	X	X	X				
contrast	X	•	X	X	X	X				
arm style	•	X	68	X	X	X	X	X	X	
form	•	X	X	X	X	X				
midline	•	X	X	X	X	X	X	X		
x height	X	•	X	X						

ABCDEFGH
IJKLMNOP
QRSTUVW
XYZ
abcdefghijkl
mnopqr
stuvwxyz
1234567890.,;
:'' &!?$

Cartier 48 point

ABCDEFGHIJKL
MNOPQRSTUV
WXYZ
abcdefghijklmnopqrs
tuvwxyz
1234567890.,;:''&!?
$

Cartier Italic 36 point

Supplier	Compugraphic 8400 Digital Typesetter
Usage	Text, Display
Similar Fonts	Michelangelo
Available Media	
Photo, Digital	
Alternate Names	

	1	2	3	4	5	6	7	8	9	0
serif	20	●	92	129	X	160	X	X	X	X
proportion	●	71	X	X	X	X				
contrast	X	●	X	X	X	X				
arm style	●	X	68	X	X	X	X	X	X	
form	X	●	X	X	X	X				
midline	X	X	X	X	●	X	X	X		
x height	X	●	X	X						

ABCDEFGH
IJKLMNOP
QRSTUVW
XYZ
abcdefghijk
lmnopqr
stuvwxyz
123456789
0.,;:''&!?$

Candida Regular 48 point

ABCDEFGHIJKLMN
OPQRSTUVWXYZ
abcdefghijklmnopqr
stuvwxyz
1234567890.,;:''&!?$

Candida Regular Italic 22 point

ABCDEFGHIJKLMN
OPQRSTUVWXYZ
abcdefghijklmnopqrs
tuvwxyz
1234567890.,;:''&!?$

Candida Bold 22 point

Supplier	**Compugraphic 8400 Digital Typesetter**
Usage	**Text, Display**
Similar Fonts	
Available Media	
Photo, Digital	
Alternate Names	

	1	2	3	4	5	6	7	8	9	0
serif	23	●	93	X	X	X	168	X	219	X
proportion	●	72	79	X	X	X				
contrast	65	●	X	X	X	X				
arm style	66	X	●	X	X	X	X	X	X	
form	●	X	X	X	X	X				
midline	X	●	X	X	X	X	X	X		
x height	X	X	●	X						

ABCDEF GHIJKLM NOPQRS TUVWXY abcdefghij klmnopqrs tuvwxyz 1234567 890.,;"&!?$

Stymie Medium 48 point

PANOSE abegmoqst

Stymie Light 24 point

PANOSE abegmoqst

Stymie Light Italic 24 point

PANOSE abegmoqst

Stymie Medium Italic 24 point

PANOSE abegmoqs

Stymie Bold 24 point

PANOSE abegmoqst

Stymie Bold Italic 24 point

PANOSE abegmoq

Stymie Extra Bold 24 point

PANOSE abegmo

Stymie Extra Bold Italic 24 point'

Supplier	**Alphatype CRS Digital Typesetter**
Usage	**Display**
Similar Fonts	**Antelope**
Available Media	
Digital, Photo, Hot, Bit	
Alternate Names	
Geometric Slabserif 711(BS), Memphis(Merg), Cairo(HC), Pyramid(IBM), ST(Itek), Karnak(Ludlow), Alexandria(Wang), A&S Gallatin	

	1	2	3	4	5	6	7	8	9	0
serif	X	•	96	X	X	X	171	214	220	237
proportion	•	77	83	X	87	X				
contrast	X	X	X	X	X	•				
arm style	X	X	X	X	X	X	•	X	X	
form	•	X	X	X	X	X				
midline	•	X	X	X	X	X	X	X		
x height	X	•	70	X						

ABCDEFG HIJKLMN OPQRSTU VWXYZ abcdefg hijklmno pqrstuvw xyz 12345 67890.,; '&!?$

ITC Lubalin Graph Medium 48 point

PANOSE abegmoqst
ITC Lubalin Graph Extra Light 24 point

PANOSE abegmoqst
ITC Lubalin Graph Extra Light Oblique 24 point

PANOSE abegmoqst
ITC Lubalin Graph Book 24 point

PANOSE abegmoqst
ITC Lubalin Graph Book Oblique 24 point

PANOSE abegmoq
ITC Lubalin Graph Medium Oblique 24 point

PANOSE abegmoq
ITC Lubalin Graph Demi 24 point

PANOSE abegmoq
ITC Lubalin Graph Demi Oblique 24 point

PANOSE abegmoqs
ITC Lubalin Graph Bold 24 point

PANOSE abegmoq
ITC Lubalin Graph Bold Oblique 24 point

Supplier	Alphatype CRS Digital Typesetter
Usage	Display
Similar Fonts	
Available Media	
Digital, Photo, DT, Bit, PS	
Alternate Names	
Geometric Slabserif 761(BS)	

	1	2	3	4	5	6	7	8	9	0
serif	X	•	96	X	X	X	171	214	**220**	237
proportion	•	77	83	X	87	X				
contrast	X	X	X	X	X	•				
arm style	X	X	X	X	X	X	•	X	X	
form	•	X	X	X	X	X				
midline	•	X	X	X	X	X	X	X		
x height	X	69	•	X						

ABCDEFG HIJKLMN OPQRSTU VWXYZ abcdefghijk lmnopqrstu vwxyz 123 4567890.,; ''&!?$

Vladimir 48 point

ABCDEFGHIJKLMN OPQRSTUVWXYZ abcdefghijklmnopq rstuvwxyz 1234567890.,;''&!?$

Vladimir Italic 24 point

PANOSE abegmoqst

Vladimir Condensed 24 point

PANOSE abegmoqst

Vladimir Bold 24 point

PANOSE abegmoqst

Vladimir Bold Italic 24 point

PANOSE abegmoqst

Vladimir Bold Condensed 24 point

Supplier	Alphatype CRS Digital Typesetter
Usage	Text, Display
Similar Fonts	
Available Media	
Hot, Photo, Digital	
Alternate Names	

	1	2	3	4	5	6	7	8	9	0
serif	38	●	X	X	150	X	X	X	X	X
proportion	66	●	X	X	X	X				
contrast	X	●	X	X	X	76				
arm style	●	X	72	X	X	X	X	X	X	
form	●	X	X	X	X	X				
midline	●	X	X	X	X	X	X	X		
x height	X	X	●	X						

ABCDEF
GHIJKLM
NOPQRS
TUVWXY
abcdefghij
klmnopqrs
tuvwxyz
1234567
890.,;"&!?$

Fairmont 48 point

ABCDEFGHIJKLMN
OPQRSTUVWXYZ
abcdefghijklmnopqrst
uvwxyz
1234567890.,;"&!?$

Fairmont Italic 24 point

ABCDEFGHIJKLMN
OPQRSTUVWXYZ
abcdefghijklmnopqrst
uvwxyz
1234567890.,;"&!?$

Fairmont Bold 24 point

Supplier	**Alphatype CRS Digital Typesetter**
Usage	**Text, Display**
Similar Fonts	
Available Media	
Digital, Photo, Hot	
Alternate Names	
Fairfield	

	1	2	3	4	5	6	7	8	9	0
serif	39	●	103	134	X	163	X	X	224	X
proportion	68	●	79	X	X	X				
contrast	X	●	74	X	X	X				
arm style	71	X	●	X	X	X	X	X	X	
form	●	X	X	X	X	X				
midline	X	●	X	X	X	X	X	X		
x height	X	●	X	X						

ABCDEF
GHIJKLM
NOPQRST
UVWXYZ
abcdefghij
klmnopqr
stuvwxyz
1234567890
.,;:"&!?$

Stempel Schadow Medium 48 point

PANOSE abegmoqst
Stempel Schadow Light 24 point

PANOSE abegmoqst
Stempel Schadow Light Italic 24 point

PANOSE abegmoqst
Stempel Schadow 24 point

PANOSE abegmoqst
Stempel Schadow Italic 24 point

PANOSE abegmoqst
Stempel Schadow Medium Italic 24 point

PANOSE abegmoqst
Stempel Schadow Bold 24 point

PANOSE abegmoqst
Stempel Schadow Bold Italic 24 point

PANOSE abegmoqst
Stempel Schadow Black 24 point

PANOSE abegmoqst
Stempel Schadow Black Italic 24 point

Supplier	**Linotronic 300 Laser Typesetter**
Usage	**Text, Display**
Similar Fonts	**Schadow Werk**
Available Media	
Hot, Photo, Digital	
Alternate Names	

	1	2	3	4	5	6	7	8	9	0
serif	39	•	99	134	X	162	X	X	225	X
proportion	68	•	79	X	X	X				
contrast	X	•	74	X	X	X				
arm style	71	X	•	X	X	X	X	X	X	
form	X	•	X	X	X	X				
midline	•	X	X	X	X	X	X	X		
x height	X	•	X	X						

ABCDEFGH
IJKLMNOPQ
RSTUVW
XYZ
abcdefghijkl
mnopqrstuv
wxyz
1234567890
.,;:"&!?$

Auriga 38 point

ABCDEFGHIJKLMNO
PQRSTUVWXYZ
abcdefghijklmnopqrst
uvwxyz
1234567890.,;:"&!?$

Auriga Italic 22 point

ABCDEFGHIJKLMN
OPQRSTUVWXYZ
abcdefghijklmnopqrs
tuvwxyz
1234567890.,;:"&!?$

Auriga Bold 22 point

Supplier	**Linotype 202 Digital Typesetter**
Usage	**Display, Text**
Similar Fonts	
Available Media	
Hot, Photo, Digital	
Alternate Names	

	1	2	3	4	5	6	7	8	9	0
serif	(41)	•	(106)	(135)	X	164	X	X	X	X
proportion	X	•	X	X	X	X				
contrast	X	72	•	X	X	X				
arm style	X	X	•	X	75	X	X	X	X	
form	•	X	X	X	X	X				
midline	•	X	X	X	X	X	X	X		
x height	X	•	X	X						

ABCDEFG HIJKLMN OPQRSTU VWXYZ abcdefghij klmnopqrs tuvwxyz 12345678 90.,;''&!?$

Else Medium 48 point

PANOSE abegmoqst
Else Light 24 point

PANOSE abegmoqst
Else Light Italic 24 point

PANOSE abegmoqst
Else Medium Italic 24 point

PANOSE abegmoqst
Else Semi Bold 24 point

PANOSE abegmoqst
Else Semi Bold Italic 24 point

PANOSE abegmoqst
Else Bold 24 point

PANOSE abegmoqst
Else Bold Italic 24 point

Supplier	**Alphatype CRS Digital Typesetter**
Usage	**Text, Display**
Similar Fonts	
Available Media	
Photo, Digital	
Alternate Names	

	1	2	3	4	5	6	7	8	9	0
serif	47	•	112	X	X	X	X	X	X	X
proportion	X	•	X	X	X	X				
contrast	X	X	•	X	X	X				
arm style	X	X	74	X	•	X	X	X	X	
form	•	X	X	X	X	X				
midline	X	•	X	X	X	X	X	X		
x height	X	X	•	X						

ABCDEFG
HIJKLMN
OP
QRSTUVW
XYZ
abcdefghijk
lmnopqr
stuvwxyz
123456789
0.,;:'"&!?$

Geometric Light 36 point

ABCDEFGHIJKLMN
OPQRSTUVWXYZ
abcdefghijklmnopqrst
uvwxyz
1234567890.,;:'"&!?$

Geometric Light Italic 19 point

ABCDEFGHIJKLMN
OPQRSTUVWXYZ
abcdefghijklmnopqrst
uvwxyz
1234567890.,;:'"&!?$

Geometric Bold 19 point

PANOSE abegmoqst

Geometric Bold Italic 24 point

Supplier	**Compugraphic 8400 Digital Typesetter**
Usage	**Display**
Similar Fonts	
Available Media	
Photo, Digital	
Alternate Names	

	1	2	3	4	5	6	7	8	9	0
serif	X	•	X	X	X	X	179	X	X	X
proportion	X	•	81	X	86	X				
contrast	X	71	X	X	X	•				
arm style	•	X	X	X	X	X	77	X	X	
form	X	X	X	X	X	•				
midline	•	X	X	X	X	X	X	X		
x height	X	X	•	X						

ABCDEFG
HIJKLMN
OPQRSTU
VWXYZ
abcdefghij
klmnopqr
stuvwxyz
12345678
90.,;:''&!?$

Glypha 55 44 point

PANOSE abegmoqst

Glypha Thin 35 24 point

PANOSE abegmoqst

Glypha Thin Italic 36 24 point

PANOSE abegmoqst

Glypha Light 45 24 point

PANOSE abegmoqst

Glypha Light Italic 46 24 point

PANOSE abegmoqst

Glypha Italic 56 24 point

PANOSE abegmoqst

Glypha Bold 65 24 point

PANOSE abegmoqst

Glypha Bold Italic 66 24 point

PANOSE abegmoqst

Glypha Black Italic 76 24 point

Supplier	**Linotronic 202 Digital Typesetter**
Usage	**Display, Text**
Similar Fonts	**Aquarius**
Available Media	
Photo, Digital, PS	
Alternate Names	

	1	2	3	4	5	6	7	8	9	0
serif	X	•	X	X	X	X	184	X	226	X
proportion	70	•	83	X	87	X				
contrast	X	X	X	X	X	•				
arm style	76	X	X	X	X	X	•	X	X	
form	•	X	X	X	X	X				
midline	•	X	X	X	X	X	X	X		
x height	X	X	•	X						

ABCDEF
GHIJKLM
NOPQRS
TUVWXY
abcdefghij
klmnopqrs
tuvwxyz
1234567
890.,;"&!?$

Eternal Oldstyle 48 point

ABCDEFGHIJKLM
NOPQRSTUVWXYZ
abcdefghijklmnopq
rstuvwxyz
1234567890.,;"&!?$

Eternal Oldstyle Italic 24 point

ABCDEFGHIJKLM
NOPQRSTUVWXYZ
abcdefghijklmnopqrst
uvwxyz
1234567890.,;"&!?$

Eternal Oldstyle Bold 24 point

Supplier	**Alphatype CRS Digital Typesetter**
Usage	**Text, Display**
Similar Fonts	
Available Media	
Photo, Digital	
Alternate Names	

	1	2	3	4	5	6	7	8	9	0
serif	52	•	X	X	152	X	X	X	X	X
proportion	X	X	•	X	X	X				
contrast	•	X	X	X	X	81				
arm style	•	X	X	X	X	X	X	X	X	
form	•	X	X	X	X	X				
midline	•	X	X	X	X	X	X	X		
x height	X	X	•	X						

ABCDEFG HIJKLMNO PQRSTUV WXYZ abc defghijklm nopqrstuv wxyz 1234 567890., ;"&!?$

ITC Leawood Medium 48 point

PANOSE abegmoqst

ITC Leawood Book 24 point

PANOSE abegmoqst

ITC Leawood Book Italic 24 point

PANOSE abegmoqst

ITC Leawood Medium Italic 24 point

PANOSE abegmoqst

ITC Leawood Bold 24 point

PANOSE abegmoqst

ITC Leawood Bold Italic 24 point

PANOSE abegmoqs

ITC Leawood Black 24 point

PANOSE abegmoqst

ITC Leawood Black Italic 24 point

Supplier	Alphatype CRS Digital Typesetter
Usage	Text, Display
Similar Fonts	Benedictine
Available Media	
Photo, Digital	
Alternate Names	

	1	2	3	4	5	6	7	8	9	0
serif	X	•	116	X	154	166	X	X	X	X
proportion	68	72	•	X	X	X				
contrast	X	•	X	X	X	X				
arm style	X	X	•	X	80	X	X	X	X	
form	•	X	X	X	X	X				
midline	X	X	•	X	X	X	X	X		
x height	X	X	•	X						

ABCDEFG
HIJKLMN
OPQRST
UVWXYZ
abcdefghi
jklmnopq
rstuvwxyz
12345678
90.,;:"&!?$

Antikva Margaret 48 point

ABCDEFGHIJKLMN
OPQRSTUVWXYZ
abcdefghijklmnopqrs
tuvwxyz
1234567890.,;:"&!?$

Antikva Margaret Italic 24 point

ABCDEFGHIJKLMN
OPQRSTUVWXYZ
abcdefghijklmnopqr
stuvwxyz
1234567890.,;:"&!?$

Antikva Margaret Black 24 point

PANOSE abegmoqst

Antikva Margaret Light 24 point

PANOSE abegmoqst

Antikva Margaret Extra Bold 24 point

Supplier	Linotype 202 Digital Typesetter
Usage	Text, Display
Similar Fonts	
Available Media	
Hot, Photo, Digital	
Alternate Names	

	1	2	3	4	5	6	7	8	9	0
serif	X	•	123	X	X	X	X	X	231	X
proportion	X	X	•	X	X	X				
contrast	X	•	X	X	X	X				
arm style	X	X	79	X	•	X	X	X	X	
form	X	•	X	X	X	X				
midline	X	•	X	X	X	X	X	X		
x height	X	X	•	X						

ABCDEF
GHIJKLM
NOPQRS
TUVWXYZ
abcdefghi
jklmnopq
rstuvwxyz
12345678
90.,;:"&!?$

A&S Gallatin Medium 48 point

ABCDEFGHIJKLMN
OPQRSTUVWXYZ
abcdefghijklmnopqrs
tuvwxyz
1234567890.,;:"&!?$

A&S Gallatin Light 24 point

ABCDEFGHIJKLMN
OPQRSTUVWXYZ
abcdefghijklmnopq
rstuvwxyz
1234567890.,;:"&!?$

A&S Gallatin Bold 24 point

Supplier	**Linotype 202 Digital Typesetter**
Usage	**Display, Text**
Similar Fonts	**Stymie**
Available Media	
Digital	
Alternate Names	

	1	2	3	4	5	6	7	8	9	0
serif	X	•	X	X	X	X	187	X	X	X
proportion	X	76	•	X	86	X				
contrast	78	X	X	X	X	•				
arm style	•	X	X	82	X	X	83	X	X	
form	•	X	X	X	X	X				
midline	•	X	X	X	X	X	X	X		
x height	X	•	X	X						

ABCDEFGHI JKLMNOP QRSTUVWX YZ
abcdefghijkl mnopqr stuvwxyz
1234567890.,: :''&!?$

Rockwell Medium 36 point

PANOSE abegmoqst
Rockwell Light 24 point

PANOSE abegmoqst
Rockwell Light Italic 24 point

PANOSE abegmoqst
Rockwell Medium Italic 24 point

PANOSE abegmoqst
Rockwell Medium Condensed 24 point

PANOSE abegmoqst
Rockwell Bold Condensed 24 point

PANOSE abegmoqst
Rockwell Bold 24 point

PANOSE abegmoqst
Rockwell Bold Italic 24 point

PANOSE abegmoq st
Rockwell Extra Bold 24 point

Supplier	**Compugraphic 8400 Digital Typesetter**
Usage	**Display, Text**
Similar Fonts	
Available Media	
Digital, Hot, DT, Photo, Bit	
Alternate Names	
Geometric Slabserif 712(BS)	

	1	2	3	4	5	6	7	8	9	0
serif	X	•	X	X	X	X	(192)	X	232	240
proportion	X	X	•	X	X	X				
contrast	X	X	X	X	X	•				
arm style	(81)	X	X	•	X	X	(83)	X	X	
form	•	X	X	X	X	X				
midline	•	X	X	X	X	X	X	X		
x height	X	•	X	X						

ABCDEFG HIJKLMN OPQRSTU VWXYZ abcdefghi jklmnopqr stuvwxyz 123456789 0.,;:"&!?$

Memphis Medium 44 point

PANOSE abegmoqst

Memphis Light 24 point

PANOSE abegmoqst

Memphis Light Italic 24 point

PANOSE abegmoqst

Memphis Medium Italic 24 point

PANOSE abegmoqst

Memphis Bold 24 point

PANOSE abegmoqst

Memphis Bold Italic 24 point

PANOSE abegmoqst

Memphis Extra Bold 24 point

PANOSE abegmoqst

Memphis Extra Bold Italic 24 point

Supplier	Linotronic 202 Digital Typesetter
Usage	Display, Text
Similar Fonts	
Available Media	
Photo, Digital, Hot, Bit	
Alternate Names	
Geometric Slabserif 703(BS), Karnak(Ludlow), Alexandria(Wang), Stymie(Alpha, AM), Cairo(HC), Pyramid(IBM), ST(Itek)	

	1	2	3	4	5	6	7	8	9	0
serif	X	•	125	X	X	X	194	X	X	X
proportion	69	77	•	X	87	X				
contrast	X	X	X	X	X	•				
arm style	81	X	X	82	X	X	•	X	X	
form	•	X	X	X	X	X				
midline	•	X	X	X	X	X	X	X		
x height	X	•	X	X						

ABCDEF
GHIJKLM
NOPQRS
TUVWXY
abcdefghi
jklmnopq
rstuvwxy
1234567
890.,;"&!?$

Monty 55 36 point

PANOSE abegmoqst

Monty Thin 35 24 point

PANOSE abegmoqst

Monty Thin Italic 36 24 point

PANOSE abegmoqst

Monty Light 45 24 point

PANOSE abegmoqst

Monty Light Italic 46 24 point

PANOSE abegmoqst

Monty 56 24 point

PANOSE abegmoq

Monty Bold 65 24 point

PANOSE abegmo

Monty Black 75 24 point

Supplier	**Alphatype CRS Digital Typesetter**
Usage	**Display, Text**
Similar Fonts	
Available Media	
Photo, Digital, Bit	
Alternate Names	
Swiss Slabserif 722(BS), Seraphim, Sierra(CG), Serifa(Merg)	

	1	2	3	4	5	6	7	8	9	0
serif	X	•	125	X	X	X	194	X	X	X
proportion	69	77	•	X	87	X				
contrast	X	X	X	X	X	•				
arm style	81	X	X	82	X	X	•	X	X	
form	•	X	X	X	X	X				
midline	•	X	X	X	X	X	X	X		
x height	X	•	X	X						

ABCDEFGHIJKL
MNOP
QRSTUVWXYZ
abcdefghijklmn
opqrstuvwxyz
1234567890.,;:'´
&!?$

Branding Iron 48 point

ABCDEFG
HIJKLMNOP
QRSTUV WXYZ
abcdefghijklm
nopqrstuvwxyz
1234567890
.,;:'"&!?$

Playbill 48 point

Supplier	Compugraphic 8400 Digital Typesetter
Usage	Display
Similar Fonts	Figaro, Hidalgo, Old Town
Available Media	
Hot, Photo, Digital, DT	
Alternate Names	

Supplier	Linotronic 202 Digital Typesetter
Usage	Display
Similar Fonts	P. T. Barnum
Available Media	
Hot, Photo, DT	
Alternate Names	

	1	2	3	4	5	6	7	8	9	0
serif	X	●	X	X	X	X	X	X	X	X
proportion	X	X	X	X	●	X				
contrast	X	X	●	X	X	X				
arm style	X	X	X	X	X	●	X	X	X	
form	X	X	●	X	X	X				
midline	●	X	X	X	X	X	X	X		
x height	X	X	●	X						

ABCDEFGH IJKLMNOP QRSTUV WXYZ abcdefghijkl mnopqrstuv wxyz 123456789 0.,;:ˇ&!?$

City Medium 48 point

ABCDEFGHIJKLMNOPQR
STUVWXYZ
abcdefghijklmnopqrstuvw
xyz
1234567890.,;:ˇ&!?$

City Light 24 point

ABCDEFGHIJKLMNO PQRSTUVWXYZ abcdefghijklmnopqrst uvwxyz 1234567890.,;:ˇ&!?$

City Bold 24 point

Supplier	**Linotype 202 Digital Typesetter**
Usage	**Display**
Similar Fonts	**Eden**
Available Media	
Digital, DT, Hot, Bit	
Alternate Names	
Square Slabserif 711(BS)	

	1	2	3	4	5	6	7	8	9	0
serif	X	•	X	X	X	X	207	X	X	X
proportion	X	76	81	X	•	X				
contrast	X	X	X	X	X	•				
arm style	•	X	X	X	X	X	87	X	X	
form	X	X	X	•	X	X				
midline	X	•	X	X	X	X	X	X		
x height	X	X	•	X						

ABCDEFGH
IJKLMNOP
QRSTUVWX
YZ
abcdefghijkl
mnopqr
stuvwxyz
1234567890.,
;:"&!?$

Stymie Medium Condensed 48 point

ABCDEFGHIJKLMNOPQR
STUVWXYZ
abcdefghijklmnopqrstuvw
xyz
1234567890.,;:"&!?$

Stymie Light Condensed 24 point

ABCDEFGHIJKLMNOPQRSTUV
WXYZ
abcdefghijklmnopqrstuvwxyz
1234567890.,;:"&!?$

Stymie Bold Condensed 24 point

PANOSE abegmoqst

Stymie Extrabold Condensed 24 point

Supplier	Compugraphic 8400 Digital Typesetter	
Usage	**Display**	
Similar Fonts		
Available Media		
Hot, Photo, Digital, Bit		
Alternate Names		
Geometric Slabserif 711(BS), Memphis(Merg), Cairo(HC), Pyramid(IBM), ST(Itek), Karnak(Ludlow), Alexandria(Wang), A&S Gallatin		

	1	2	3	4	5	6	7	8	9	0
serif	X	•	X	X	158	X	**209**	X	X	X
proportion	**69**	77	**83**	X	•	X				
contrast	X	X	X	X	X	•				
arm style	86	X	X	X	X	X	•	X	X	
form	•	X	**88**	X	X	X				
midline	•	X	X	X	X	X	X	X		
x height	X	•	X	X						

ABCDEFG
HIJKLMNOP
QRSTUV
WXYZ
abcdefghijkl
mnopqrstuv
wxyz
1234567890.,
;:''&!?$

Memphis Medium Condensed 48 point

ABCDEFGHIJKLMNOP
QRSTUVWXYZ
abcdefghijklmnop
qrstuvwxyz
1234567890.,;:''&!?$

Memphis Bold Condensed 24 point

ABCDEFGHIJKLMNOP
QRSTUVWXYZ
abcdefghijklmnop
qrstuvwxyz
1234567890.,;:''&!?$

Memphis Extra Bold Condensed 24 point

Supplier	Linotronic 202 Digital Typesetter
Usage	Display
Similar Fonts	Karnak Obelisk, Eden
Available Media	
Photo, Digital	
Alternate Names	
Geometric Slabserif 703(BS), Karnak(Ludlow), Alexandria(Wang), Stymie(Alpha, AM), Cairo(HC), Pyramid(IBM), ST(Itek)	

	1	2	3	4	5	6	7	8	9	0
serif	X	•	X	X	158	X	209	X	X	X
proportion	69	77	83	X	•	X				
contrast	X	X	X	X	X	•				
arm style	86	X	X	X	X	X	•	X	X	
form	(87)	X	•	X	X	X				
midline	•	X	X	X	X	X	X	X		
x height	X	•	X	X						

ABCDEF
GHIJKLM
NOPQRS
TUVWXY
abcdefghi
jklmnopq
rstuvwxy
1234567
890.,;"&!?

Bramley Medium 42 point

ABCDEFGHIJKLMN
OPQRSTUVWXYZ
abcdefghijklmnopqrst
uvwxyz 1234567890
.,;"&!?$

Bramley Light 24 point

ABCDEFGHIJKLM
NOPQRSTUVWXYZ
abcdefghijklmnopq
rstuvwxyz 1234567
890.,;"&!?$

Bramley Bold 24 point

PANOSE abegmoqst

Bramley Extra Bold 24 point

Supplier	Alphatype CRS Digital Typesetter
Usage	Text, Display
Similar Fonts	Shelley
Available Media	
Photo, Digital, DT	
Alternate Names	

	1	2	3	4	5	6	7	8	9	0
serif	3	65	•	X	X	X	X	X	X	X
proportion	•	97	114	X	X	X				
contrast	•	93	95	X	X	X				
arm style	X	X	•	X	X	X	X	X	X	
form	•	X	X	X	X	X				
midline	X	X	•	X	X	X	X	X		
x height	X	•	X	X						

ABCDEFG
HIJKLMN
OPQRST
UVWXYZ
abcdefghij
klmnopqr
stuvwxyz
1234567890
.,;:'"&!?$

Palatino 48 point

ABCDEFGHIJKLMN
OPQRSTUVWXYZ
abcdefghijklm
nopqrstuvwxyz
1234567890.,;:"&!?

Palatino Italic 24 point

ABCDEFGHIJKLM
NOPQRSTUVWXYZ
abcdefghijklm
nopqrstuvwxyz
1234567890.,;:"&!?

Palatino Bold 24 point

PANOSE abegmoqs

Palatino Bold Italic 24 point

Supplier	Compugraphic 8400 Digital Typesetter
Usage	Text, Display
Similar Fonts	Weiss Roman, Compano
Available Media	
Photo, Digital, DT, Hot, Bit, PS	
Alternate Names	
Zapf Calligraphic 801(BS), Andover(AM, Auto, Dymo), Palacio(CG), Malibu(Auto), Elegante(HC), Patina(Alpha), Pontiac(Wang)	

	1	2	3	4	5	6	7	8	9	0
serif	5	66	•	129	X	160	X	X	X	X
proportion	•	X	X	X	X	X				
contrast	X	•	X	X	X	X				
arm style	•	X	93	X	X	X	X	X	X	
form	•	92	X	X	X	X				
midline	•	X	X	X	X	X	X	X		
x height	X	•	X	X						

ABCDEF GHIJKLM NOPQRS TUVWXY abcdef ghijklmno pqrstuvw xyz 12345 67890.,'&

Belwe Medium 48 point

ABCDEFGHIJKLMNO
PQRSTUVWXYZ
abcdefghijklmnopqrstu
vwxyz
1234567890.,:"&!? $

Belwe Light 24 point

ABCDEFGHIJKLMNO
PQRSTUVWXYZ
abcdefghijklmnopqrstu
vwxyz
1234567890.,:"&!? $

Belwe Condensed 24 point

PANOSE abegmoqst

Belwe Light Italic 24 point

PANOSE abegmoq

Belwe Bold 24 point

Supplier	**Alphatype CRS Digital Typesetter**
Usage	**Display, Text**
Similar Fonts	
Available Media	
Photo, Digital, DT	
Alternate Names	
Belter	

	1	2	3	4	5	6	7	8	9	0
serif	(16)	66	•	130	X	160	X	X	X	X
proportion	•	X	X	X	X	X				
contrast	X	•	X	X	X	X				
arm style	•	X	93	X	X	X	X	X	X	
form	•	X	X	X	X	X				
midline	X	X	•	X	X	X	X	X		
x height	X	X	•	X						

ABCDEFGH
IJKLMNOP
QRSTUVW
XYZ
abcdefghijk
lmnopqr
stuvwxyz
1234567890.
,;:''&!?$

Raleigh Medium 42 point

ABCDEFGHIJKLMN
OPQRSTUVWXYZ
abcdefghijklmnopqr
stuvwxyz
1234567890.,;:''&!?$

Raleigh Demi Bold 24 point

PANOSE abegmoqst

Raleigh Light 24 point

PANOSE abegmoqst

Raleigh Regular 24 point

PANOSE abegmoqst

Raleigh Bold 24 point

PANOSE abegmoqst

Raleigh Extrabold 24 point

Supplier	Compugraphic 8400 Digital Typesetter
Usage	Display, Text
Similar Fonts	Cartier
Available Media	
Photo, Digital, DT	
Alternate Names	

	1	2	3	4	5	6	7	8	9	0
serif	(20)	67	•	129	X	160	X	X	X	X
proportion	•	X	X	X	X	X				
contrast	X	•	X	X	X	X				
arm style	•	X	93	X	X	X	X	X	X	
form	(90)	•	X	X	X	X				
midline	•	X	X	X	X	X	X	X		
x height	X	•	X	X						

ABCDEFG
HIJKLMN
OPQRSTU
VWXYZ
abcdefghijkl
mnopqrstuv
wxyz 1234
567890
.,;"&!?$

Cheltenham Medium 48 point

ABCDEFGHIJKLMNO
PQRSTUVWXYZ abcd
efghijklmnopqrstuvwxyz
1234567890.,;"&!?$

Cheltenham Old Style Italic 24 point

PANOSE abegmoqst

Cheltenham Old Style 24 point

PANOSE abegmoqst

Cheltenham Medium Italic 24 point

PANOSE abegmoqst

Cheltenham Old Style Condensed 24 point

PANOSE abegmoqst

Cheltenham Bold 24 point

Supplier	Alphatype CRS Digital Typesetter
Usage	Display, Text
Similar Fonts	Sorbonne, Chelsea
Available Media	
Hot, DT, Digital, Bit	
Alternate Names	
Stubserif 205(BS), Cheltonian(HC), Gloucester, Nordhoff(Auto), Winchester	

	1	2	3	4	5	6	7	8	9	0
serif	23	68	•	X	X	X	168	X	219	X
proportion	•	99	116	X	126	X				
contrast	89	•	95	X	X	X				
arm style	90	X	•	X	X	X	X	X	X	
form	•	X	X	X	X	X				
midline	•	X	X	X	X	X	X	X		
x height	•	X	94	X						

ABCDEFG HIJKLMN OPQRSTU VWXYZ abcdefghij klmnopqr stuvwxyz 1234567 890.,;"&!?

Cardinal Medium 48 point

ABCDEFGHIJKLMN OPQRSTUVWXYZ abcdefghijklmnopqr stuvwxyz 1234567890.,;"&!?$

Cardinal Medium Italic 24 point

PANOSE abegmoqst

Cardinal Light 24 point

PANOSE abegmoqst

Cardinal Light Italic 24 point

PANOSE abegmoqst

Cardinal Demibold 24 point

PANOSE abegmoq

Cardinal Bold 24 point

Supplier	Alphatype CRS Digital Typesetter
Usage	Text, Display
Similar Fonts	
Available Media	
Digital	
Alternate Names	

	1	2	3	4	5	6	7	8	9	0
serif	23	68	•	X	X	X	168	X	219	X
proportion	•	(102)	(118)	X	126	X				
contrast	89	•	95	X	X	X				
arm style	90	X	•	X	X	X	X	X	X	
form	•	X	X	X	X	X				
midline	•	X	X	X	X	X	X	X		
x height	(93)	X	•	X						

ABCDEFG HIJKLMNO PQRSTUV WXYZ abcd efghijklmno pqrstuvwxy 1234567 890.,;"&!?$

Caledonia 48 point

ABCDEFGHIJKLM NOPQRSTUVWXYZ abcdefghijklmnopqrs tuvwxyz 1234567890 .,;"&!?$

Caledonia Italic 24 point

ABCDEFGHIJKLMNO PQRSTUVWXYZ abcdefg hijklmnopqrstuvwxyz 1234567890.,;"&!?$

Caledonia Bold 24 point

PANOSE abegmoqst

Caledonia Bold Italic 24 point

Supplier	**Alphatype CRS Digital Typesetter**
Usage	**Text, Display**
Similar Fonts	**Wandsworth**
Available Media	
Photo, Digital, Hot, Bit	
Alternate Names	
Transitional 511(BS), Gemini, California(CG), Caledo(Alpha), Cornelia, Edinburg(Wang), Gale(III), Highland(Auto, Dymo), Laurel(HC)	

	1	2	3	4	5	6	7	8	9	0
serif	(31)	X	•	(131)	X	(161)	X	X	X	X
proportion	•	(109)	X	X	127	X				
contrast	89	93	•	X	X	X				
arm style	X	X	•	X	X	X	X	X	X	
form	•	X	X	X	X	X				
midline	X	•	X	X	X	X	X	X		
x height	X	•	X	X						

ABCDEF GHIJKLM NOPQRST UVWXYZ abcdefghij klmnopqr stuvwxyz 123456789 0.,;:"&!?$

Beton Bold 48 point

ABCDEFGHIJKLM
NOPQRSTUVWXYZ
abcdefghijklm
nopqrstuvwxyz
1234567890.,;:"&!?$

Beton Bold Condensed 24 point

ABCDEFGHIJKLM
NOPQRSTUVWXYZ
abcdefghijklm
nopqrstuvwxyz
1234567890.,;:"&!?$

Beton Extra Bold 24 point

Supplier	Linotype 300 Laser Typesetter
Usage	Display
Similar Fonts	Girder, Butress
Available Media	
Hot, Photo, Digital, Hot, DT	
Alternate Names	

	1	2	3	4	5	6	7	8	9	0
serif	X	69	•	X	X	X	171	214	220	237
proportion	•	X	125	X	X	X				
contrast	X	X	X	X	X	•				
arm style	X	X	X	X	X	X	•	X	X	
form	•	X	X	X	X	X				
midline	•	X	X	X	X	X	X	X		
x height	X	•	X	X						

ABCDEFG
HIJKLMNO
PQRSTUV
WXYZ abc
defghijklm
nopqrstuv
wxyz 1234
567890.,
;"&!?$

ITC Italia Medium 48 Point

ABCDEFGHIJKLMNOP
QRSTUVWXYZ
abcdefghijklmnopqrst
uvwxyz
1234567890.,;"&!?$

ITC Italia Book 24 point

ABCDEFGHIJKLMNO
PQRSTUVWXYZ
abcdefghijklmnop
qrstuvwxyz
1234567890.,;"&!?$

ITC Italia Bold 24 point

Supplier	Alphatype CRS Digital Typesetter
Usage	Display, Text
Similar Fonts	Masterdon (bold), Antique No.3 (light)
Available Media	
Digital, Photo, DT, Bit	
Alternate Names	
Revival 791(BS)	

	1	2	3	4	5	6	7	8	9	0
serif	X	X	•	X	X	X	177	X	X	X
proportion	89	•	113	X	X	X				
contrast	•	99	106	X	X	X				
arm style	X	X	•	X	X	X	X	X	X	
form	•	98	X	X	X	X				
midline	•	X	X	X	X	X	X	X		
x height	X	•	X	X						

ABCDEFGHI JKLMNOPQ RSTUVWXY abcdefghijk lmnopqrstu vwxyz 123 4567890 .,;"&!?$

Congress Medium 48 point

ABCDEFGHIJKLMNOPQ RSTUVWXYZ abcdefghi jklmnopqrstuvwxyz 1234567890.,;"&!?$

Congress Regular 24 point

ABCDEFGHIJKLMNOPQ RSTUVWXYZ abcdefghij klmnopqrstuvwxyz 1234567890.,;"&!?$

Congress Regular Italic 24 point

PANOSE abegmoqst

Congress Bold 24 point

PANOSE abegmoqst

Congress Heavy 24 point

Supplier	Alphatype CRS Digital Typesetter
Usage	Text, Display
Similar Fonts	
Available Media	
Photo, Digital	
Alternate Names	

	1	2	3	4	5	6	7	8	9	0
serif	X	X	•	X	X	X	177	X	X	X
proportion	89	•	115	X	X	X				
contrast	•	99	106	X	X	X				
arm style	X	X	•	X	X	X	X	X	X	
form	(97)	•	X	X	X	X				
midline	•	X	X	X	X	X	X	X		
x height	X	•	X	X						

ABCDEFG HIJKLMN OPQRSTU VWXYZ abcdefghij klmnopqrs tuvwxyz 1234567 890.,;"&!?

Century Old Style 48 point

ABCDEFGHIJKLMN OPQRSTUVWXYZ abcdefghijklmnopqrstu vwxyz 1234567890 .,;"&!?$

Century Old Style Italic 24 point

ABCDEFGHIJKLM NOPQRSTUVWXYZ abcdefghijklmnopqr stuvwxyz 1234567890.,;"&!?$

Century Old Style Bold 24 point

Supplier	**Alphatype CRS Digital Typesetter**
Usage	**Text, Display**
Similar Fonts	**Berner**
Available Media	
Digital, Photo, Hot, PS, Bit	
Alternate Names	
Cambridge Old Style(Wang), Revival 707(BS)	

	1	2	3	4	5	6	7	8	9	0
serif	39	72	•	**134**	X	162	X	X	224	X
proportion	93	•	(116)	X	(126)	X				
contrast	(97)	•	(106)	X	X	X				
arm style	X	X	•	X	X	X	X	X	X	
form	•	X	X	X	X	X				
midline	•	(103)	X	X	X	X	X	X		
x height	X	•	(102)	X						

ABCDEFG
HIJKLMN
OPQRSTU
VWXYZ
abcdefghi
jklmnopq
rstuvwxyz
12345678
90.,;:
"&!?$

Egyptienne Frutiger 55 48 point

ABCDEFGHIJKLMN
OPQRSTUVWXYZ
abcdefghijklmnopq
rstuvwxyz
1234567890.,;:"&!?$

Egyptienne Frutiger Italic 56 24 point

ABCDEFGHIJKLMNOPQ
RSTUVWXYZ
abcdefghijklmnopqrstuvw
xyz
1234567890.,;:"&!?$

Egyptienne Frutiger Bold Condensed 67 24 point

PANOSE abegmoqst

Egyptienne Frutiger Bold 65 24 point

PANOSE abegmoqst

Egyptienne Frutiger Black 75 24 point

Supplier	**Linotype 202 Digital Typesetter**
Usage	**Display, Text**
Similar Fonts	**Aachen, Bismark**
Available Media	
Hot, Photo, Digital, DT, Bit	
Alternate Names	
Humanist Slabserif 712(BS), Egyptienne	

	1	2	3	4	5	6	7	8	9	0
serif	39	72	•	(134)	X	162	X	X	224	X
proportion	93	•	(116)	X	(126)	X				
contrast	(97)	•	(106)	X	X	X				
arm style	X	X	•	X	X	X	X	X	X	
form	•	X	X	X	X	X				
midline	•	(103)	X	X	X	X	X	X		
x height	X	•	(102)	X						

ABCDEFG
HIJKLMN
OPQRSTU
VWXYZ
abcdefghijk
lmnopqrstu
vwxyz
1234567890.
,;:''&!?$

Textype 40 point

ABCDEFGHIJKLM
NOPQRSTUVWXYZ
abcdefghijklmnopqr
stuvwxyz
1234567890.,;:''&!?$

Textype Italic 24 point

ABCDEFGHIJKLM
NOPQRSTUVWXYZ
abcdefghijklmnopqrs
tuvwxyz
1234567890.,;:''&!?$

Textype Bold 24 point

PANOSE abegmoqst

Textype Bold Italic 24 point

Supplier	**Linotronic 202 Digital Typesetter**
Usage	**Text, Display**
Similar Fonts	**Lectura, Egizio**
Available Media	
Photo, Digital, Bit	
Alternate Names	
Century 731(BS)	

	1	2	3	4	5	6	7	8	9	0
serif	39	72	•	(134)	X	162	X	X	224	X
proportion	93	•	(116)	X	(126)	X				
contrast	(97)	•	(106)	X	X	X				
arm style	X	X	•	X	X	X	X	X	X	
form	•	X	X	X	X	X				
midline	•	(103)	X	X	X	X	X	X		
x height	X	•	(102)	X						

ABCDEFG
HIJKLMNO
PQRSTUV
WXYZ abc
defghijklm
nopqrstuv
wxyz 1234
567890
.,;"'&!?$

ITC Cheltenham Book 48 point

PANOSE abegmoqst

ITC Cheltenham Light 24 point

PANOSE abegmoqst

ITC Cheltenham Light Italic 24 point

PANOSE abegmoqst

ITC Cheltenham Book Italic 24 point

PANOSE abegmoqst

ITC Cheltenham Bold 24 point

PANOSE abegmoqst

ITC Cheltenham Bold Italic 24 point

PANOSE abegmo

ITC Cheltenham Ultra 24 point

PANOSE abegmo

ITC Cheltenham Ultra Italic 24 point

Supplier	**Alphatype CRS Digital Typesetter**
Usage	**Text, Display**
Similar Fonts	
Available Media	
Digital, Photo, DT, Bit, PS	
Alternate Names	
Stubserif 705(BS), Cheltonian(HC), Gloucester, Nordhoff(Auto), Winchester	

	1	2	3	4	5	6	7	8	9	0
serif	39	72	•	134	X	162	X	X	224	X
proportion	94	•	118	X	126	X				
contrast	97	•	108	X	X	X				
arm style	X	X	•	X	X	X	X	X	X	
form	•	X	X	X	X	X				
midline	•	104	X	X	X	X	X	X		
x height	X	99	•	X						

ABCDEF
GHIJKLM
OPQRSTU
VWXYZ
abcdefghij
klmnopqrs
tuvwxyz
1234567
890.,;"&!?$

Concert 48 point

ABCDEFGHIJKLMNO
PQRSTUVWXYZ
abcdefghijklmnopqrstu
vwxyz
1234567890.,;:"&!?$

Concert Italic 24 point

ABCDEFGHIJKLMN
OPQRSTUVWXYZ
abcdefghijklmnopqrs
tuvwxyz
1234567890.,;"&!?$

Concert Bold 24 point

Supplier	Alphatype CRS Digital Typesetter
Usage	Text
Similar Fonts	Bauer Classic, Caslon Old Face 2
Available Media	
Photo, Digital	
Alternate Names	
Concorde(Merg)	

	1	2	3	4	5	6	7	8	9	0
serif	(39)	**72**	•	134	X	**163**	X	X	224	X
proportion	93	•	122	X	126	X				
contrast	97	•	(109)	X	X	X				
arm style	X	X	•	X	X	X	X	X	X	
form	•	X	X	X	X	X				
midline	(99)	•	X	X	X	X	X	X		
x height	X	•	(104)	X						

ABCDEFG HIJKLMN OPQRSTU VWXYZ abcdefghi jklmnopq rstuvwxyz 12345678 90.,;:''&!?$

Dominante 48 point

ABCDEFGHIJKLMNO PQRSTUVWXYZ abcdefghijklmnopqrs tuvwxyz 1234567890.,;:''&!?$

Dominante Italic 24 point

ABCDEFGHIJKLMN OPQRSTUVWXYZ abcdefghijklmnopqr stuvwxyz 1234567890.,;:''&!?$

Dominante Bold 24 point

Supplier	**Linotype 202 Digital Typesetter**
Usage	**Text, Display**
Similar Fonts	
Available Media	
Hot, Photo, Digital, Hot	
Alternate Names	

	1	2	3	4	5	6	7	8	9	0
serif	39	72	•	134	X	163	X	X	224	X
proportion	93	•	(122)	X	126	X				
contrast	97	•	109	X	X	X				
arm style	X	X	•	X	X	X	X	X	X	
form	•	X	X	X	X	X				
midline	(102)	•	X	X	X	X	X	X		
x height	X	(103)	•	X						

ABCDEF
GHIJKLM
NOPQRS
TUVWXY
abcdefghijk
lmnopqrstu
vwxyz 1234
567890.,
;"&!?$

Plantin 48 point

ABCDEFGHIJKLM
NOPQRSTUVWXYZ
abcdefghijklmnopqrstuv
wxyz
1234567890.,;:''&!?$

Plantin Italic 23 point

PANOSE abegmoqst

Plantin Light 24 point

PANOSE abegmoqst

Plantin Light Italic 24 point

PANOSE abegmoqst

Plantin Bold 24 point

PANOSE abegmoqst

Plantin Bold Italic 24 point

Supplier	Alphatype CRS Digital Typesetter
Usage	Text, Display
Similar Fonts	
Available Media	
Digital, DT, Photo, Bit	
Alternate Names	
Aldine 721(BS), PL(Itek), Atlantic(Alpha), Planet(Wang)	

	1	2	3	4	5	6	7	8	9	0
serif	40	X	•	X	(151)	X	X	X	X	X
proportion	X	•	X	X	X	X				
contrast	X	X	•	X	X	X				
arm style	•	X	(108)	X	110	X	X	X	X	
form	•	X	X	X	X	X				
midline	•	X	X	X	X	X	X	X		
x height	X	X	•	X						

ABCDEFGHIJ KLMNOP QRSTUVWX YZ abcdefghijkl mnopqr stuvwxyz 1234567890. ,;:''&!?$

Accolade Medium 36 point

ABCDEFGHIJKLMN
OPQRSTUVWXYZ
abcdefghijklmnop
qrstuvwxyz
1234567890.,;:''&!?$

Accolade Light 24 point

*ABCDEFGHIJKLMNO
PQRSTUVWXYZ
abcdefghijklmnopqr
stuvwxyz
1234567890.,;:''&!?$*

Accolade Light Italic 23 point

PANOSE abegmoqst

Accolade Bold 24 point

Supplier	**Compugraphic 8400 Digital Typesetter**
Usage	**Text, Display**
Similar Fonts	
Available Media	
Digital, Photo	
Alternate Names	

	1	2	3	4	5	6	7	8	9	0
serif	(41)	(74)	•	(135)	X	164	X	X	X	X
proportion	95	•	X	X	127	X				
contrast	(97)	(99)	•	X	X	X				
arm style	105	X	•	X	110	X	X	X	X	
form	•	X	X	X	X	X				
midline	•	(109)	X	X	X	X	X	X		
x height	X	•	(108)	X						

ABCDEFG HIJKLMN OPQRSTU VWXYZ abcdefghij klmnopqrs tuvwxyz 12 34567890 .,;"&!?$

Astro 48 point

ABCDEFGHIJKLMN OPQRSTUVWXYZ abcdefghijklmnopqrst uvwxyz 1234567890 .,;"&!?$

Astro Italic 24 point

ABCDEFGHIJKLMN OPQRSTUVWXYZ abcdefghijklmnopqrst uvwxyz 1234567890.,;"&!?$

Astro Bold 24 point

Supplier	Alphatype CRS Digital Typesetter	
Usage	Text, Display	
Similar Fonts	Corolla	
Available Media		
Digital, Hot, DT, Bit		
Alternate Names		
Dutch 823(BS), Aztec(Auto), Aster(Merg, CG)		

	1	2	3	4	5	6	7	8	9	0
serif	(41)	(74)	•	(135)	X	164	X	X	X	X
proportion	95	•	X	X	127	X				
contrast	(97)	(99)	•	X	X	X				
arm style	105	X	•	X	110	X	X	X	X	
form	•	X	X	X	X	X				
midline	•	(109)	X	X	X	X	X	X		
x height	X	•	(108)	X						

ABCDEFG HIJKLMN OPQRSTU VWXYZ abcdefghij klmnopqr stuvwxyz 12345678 90.,;''&!?$

Criterion Medium 48 point

ABCDEFGHIJKLMNO PQRSTUVWXYZ abcdefghijklmnopqrs tuvwxyz 1234567890.,;''&!?$

Criterion Book Italic 24 point

PANOSE abegmoqst

Criterion Light 24 point

PANOSE abegmoqst

Criterion Light Italic 24 point

PANOSE abegmoqst

Criterion Book 24 point

PANOSE abegmoqst

Criterion Bold 24 point

Supplier	**Alphatype CRS Digital Typesetter**
Usage	**Text, Display**
Similar Fonts	
Available Media	
Photo, Digital	
Alternate Names	

	1	2	3	4	5	6	7	8	9	0
serif	(43)	74	•	135	X	164	X	X	X	X
proportion	95	•	X	X	(127)	X				
contrast	97	(102)	•	X	X	X				
arm style	(105)	X	•	X	110	X	X	X	X	
form	•	X	X	X	X	X				
midline	•	X	X	X	X	X	X	X		
x height	X	(106)	•	X						

ABCDEFG HIJKLMN OPQRSTU VWXYZ abcdefghij klmnopqrs tuvwxyz 1234567 890.,;"&!?

Century Schoolbook 48 point

ABCDEFGHIJKLM NOPQRSTUVWXYZ abcdefghijklmnopqr stuvwxyz 1234567890.,;"&!?$

Century Schoolbook Italic 24 point

ABCDEFGHIJKLM NOPQRSTUVWXYZ abcdefghijklmnopqr stuvwxyz 1234567890.,;"&!?$

Century Schoolbook Bold 24 point

PANOSE abegmoqst

Century Schoolbook Bold Italic 24 point

Supplier	**Alphatype CRS Digital Typesetter**
Usage	**Text, Display**
Similar Fonts	
Available Media	
Digital, Photo, Hot, DT, Bit	
Alternate Names	
Cambridge Schoolbook(Wang), Century Medium(IBM), Century Modern, Century Textbook(CG), CS(Itek), Schoolbook, Century Text(Alpha), Century 702(BS)	

	1	2	3	4	5	6	7	8	9	0
serif	(44)	74	•	135	X	(164)	X	X	X	X
proportion	(95)	•	X	X	127	X				
contrast	97	(103)	•	X	X	X				
arm style	105	X	•	X	(110)	X	X	X	X	
form	•	X	X	X	X	X				
midline	(106)	•	X	X	X	X	X	X		
x height	X	•	X	X						

ABCDEFGH IJKLMNOP QRSTUVWX YZ abcdefghijklm nopqr stuvwxyz 1234567890.,;: '&!?$

Century Expanded 36 point

ABCDEFGHIJKLM NOPQRSTUVWXYZ abcdefghijklmnopqrst uvwxyz 1234567890.,;:''&!?$

Century Expanded Italic 23 point

ABCDEFGHIJKLM NOPQRSTUVWXYZ abcdefghijklmnopqr stuvwxyz 1234567890.,;:''&!?$

Century Expanded Bold 23 point

PANOSE abegmoqst

Century Expanded Bold Italic 24 point

Supplier	Compugraphic 8400 Digital Typesetter
Usage	Display, Text
Similar Fonts	
Available Media	
Hot, Photo, Digital, Bit	
Alternate Names	
Century 701(BS)	

	1	2	3	4	5	6	7	8	9	0
serif	(46)	75	•	X	X	X	X	X	X	X
proportion	X	•	X	X	X	X				
contrast	X	X	•	X	X	X				
arm style	105	X	(109)	X	•	X	X	X	X	
form	•	X	X	X	X	X				
midline	X	•	X	X	X	X	X	X		
x height	X	•	(112)	X						

ABCDEF
GHIJKLM
NOPQRS
TUVWXYZ
abcdefghij
kmnopqrst
uvwxyz
123456789
0.,;:"&!?$

New Century Schoolbook 48 point

PANOSE abegmoqst
New Century Schoolbook Italic 24 point

PANOSE abegmoqst
New Century Schoolbook SemiBold 24 point

PANOSE abegmoqst
New Century Schoolbook SemiBold Italic 24 point

PANOSE abegmoqst
New Century Schoolbook Bold 24 point

PANOSE abegmoqst
New Century Schoolbook Bold Italic 24 point

PANOSE abegmoqst
New Century Schoolbook Black 24 point

PANOSE abegmoqst
New Century Schoolbook Black Italic 24 point

Supplier	Linotype 202 Digital Typesetter
Usage	Text, Display
Similar Fonts	
Available Media	
Photo, Digital, PS	
Alternate Names	
Cambridge Schoolbook(Wang), Century Medium(IBM), Century Modern, Century Textbook(CG), CS(Itek), Schoolbook, Century Text(Alpha), Century 702(BS)	

	1	2	3	4	5	6	7	8	9	0
serif	(46)	75	•	X	X	X	X	X	X	X
proportion	X	•	X	X	X	X				
contrast	X	X	•	X	X	X				
arm style	105	X	(109)	X	•	X	X	X	X	
form	•	X	X	X	X	X				
midline	X	•	X	X	X	X	X	X		
x height	X	•	(112)	X						

ABCDEFG HIJKLMN OPQRSTU VWXYZ abcdefghij klmnopqr stuvwxyz 123456789 0.,;:''&!?$

Corona 40 point

ABCDEFGHIJKLMNO PQRSTUVWXYZ abcdefghijklmnopqrs tuvwxyz 1234567890.,;:''&!?$

Corona Italic 24 point

ABCDEFGHIJKL MNOPQRSTUVW XYZ abcdefghijklmnop qrstuvwxyz 1234567890.,;:''&!?$

Corona Bold Face No. 2 24 point

Supplier	**Linotype 202 Digital Typesetter**
Usage	**Text, Display**
Similar Fonts	**Congress**
Available Media	
Photo, Digital, Bit	
Alternate Names	
Aquarius, CR(Itek), News 705(BS), Newstext, Crown(AM, Dymo), Koronna(Alpha), Nimbus, Royal, News No. 3,5,6(CG), Quincy, Royal, Vela	

	1	2	3	4	5	6	7	8	9	0
serif	(47)	(75)	•	X	X	X	X	X	X	X
proportion	X	•	X	X	X	X				
contrast	X	X	•	X	X	X				
arm style	105	X	109	X	•	X	X	X	X	
form	•	X	X	X	X	X				
midline	X	•	X	X	X	X	X	X		
x height	X	110	•	X						

ABCDEF
GHIJKLM
NOPQRST
UVWXYZ
abcdefgh
ijklmnop
qrstuvwx
yz12345
67890.,;''
&!?

Quint Medium 48 point

ABCDEFGHIJKLMN
OPQRSTUVWXYZ
abcdefghijklmnopqrs
tuvwxyz
1234567890.,;:"&!?$

Quint Medium Italic 24 point

PANOSE abegmoqst

Quint Light 24 point

PANOSE abegmoqst

Quint Light Italic 24 point

PANOSE abegmoq

Quint Bold 24 point

PANOSE abegmo

Quint Extrabold 24 point

Supplier	**Alphatype CRS Digital Typesetter**
Usage	**Text, Display**
Similar Fonts	**Deliverance**
Available Media	
Photo, Digital	
Alternate Names	

	1	2	3	4	5	6	7	8	9	0
serif	X	X	•	X	X	(165)	X	X	(230)	X
proportion	89	97	•	X	X	X				
contrast	•	(118)	X	124	X	X				
arm style	X	X	•	X	X	X	X	X	X	
form	•	(115)	X	X	X	X				
midline	•	X	X	X	X	X	X	X		
x height	X	X	•	X						

ABCDEF
GHIJKLM
NOPQRS
TUVWXYZ
abcdefghij
klmnopqrs
tuvwxyz
1234567
890.,;''&!?$

ITC Korinna 48 point

PANOSE abegmoqst

ITC Korinna Kursiv 24 point

PANOSE abegmoqs

ITC Korinna Bold 24 point

PANOSE abegmoqs

ITC Korinna Kursiv Bold 24 point

PANOSE abegmoq

ITC Korinna Extra Bold 24 point

PANOSE abegmoq

ITC Korinna Kursive Extra Bold 24 point

PANOSE abegmo

ITC Korinna Heavy 24 point

PANOSE abegmo

ITC Korinna Kursive Heavy 24 point

Supplier	Alphatype CRS Digital Typesetter
Usage	Display, Text
Similar Fonts	
Available Media	
Digital, Photo, DT, Bit, PS	
Alternate Names	
Stubserif 711(BS), Kordova(Wang)	

	1	2	3	4	5	6	7	8	9	0
serif	X	X	●	X	X	165	X	X	230	X
proportion	89	97	●	X	X	X				
contrast	●	116	X	124	X	X				
arm style	X	X	●	X	X	X	X	X	X	
form	●	X	X	X	X	X				
midline	X	X	●	X	X	X	X	X		
x height	X	●	X	X						

ABCDEFGHI JKLMNOP QRSTUVWX YZ abcdefghijkl mnopqr stuvwxyz 1234567890 .,;:'`&!?$

Egyptian No. 505 42 point

ABCDEFGHIJKLMNO
PQRSTUVWXYZ
abcdefghijklmnopqrs
tuvwxyz
1234567890.,;:'`&!?$

Egyptian No. 505 Medium 24 point

**ABCDEFGHIJKLMNOPQ
RSTUVWXYZ
abcdefghijklmnopqrstu
vwxyz
1234567890.,;:''&!?$**

Egyptian No. 505 Bold 24 point

PANOSE abegmoqst

Egyptian No. 505 Light 24 point

PANOSE abegmoqst

Egyptian No. 505 Bold Condensed 24 point

Supplier	**Compugraphic 8400 Digital Typesetter**
Usage	**Display**
Similar Fonts	**Impressum**
Available Media	
Hot, Photo, Digital	
Alternate Names	

	1	2	3	4	5	6	7	8	9	0
serif	X	X	●	X	X	165	X	X	230	X
proportion	89	98	●	X	X	X				
contrast	●	116	X	124	X	X				
arm style	X	X	●	X	X	X	X	X	X	
form	(113)	●	X	X	X	X				
midline	●	X	X	X	X	X	X	X		
x height	X	X	●	X						

ABCDEFG HIJKLMN OPQRSTU VWXYZ abcdefghij klmnopqrs tuvwxyz 123456789 0.,;:''&!?$

Clarendon 40 point

ABCDEFGHIJKLMNOPQR STUVWXYZ abcdefghijklmnopqrstuv wxyz 1234567890.,;:''&!?$

Clarendon Bold Condensed 24 point

PANOSE abegmoqst

Clarendon Light 24 point

PANOSE abegmoqst

Clarendon Condensed 24 point

PANOSE abegmoqst

Clarendon Heavy 24 point

PANOSE abegmoqst

Clarendon Bold 24 point

PANOSE abegmoqst

Clarendon Black 24 point

Supplier	Linotype 202 Digital Typesetter
Usage	Display
Similar Fonts	Remy
Available Media	
Digital, DT, Photo, Hot, Bit	
Alternate Names	
Clarendon 701(BS), Clarion(Auto), Clarique(HC), Craw Clarendon(Alpha, CG)	

	1	2	3	4	5	6	7	8	9	0
serif	X	79	•	X	153	166	X	X	X	X
proportion	93	99	•	X	126	X				
contrast	113	•	X	124	X	X				
arm style	X	X	•	X	123	X	X	X	X	
form	•	X	X	X	X	X				
midline	•	X	X	X	X	X	X	X		
x height	X	•	118	X						

ABCDEFGH IJKLMNOP QRSTUVWX YZ
abcdefghijk lmnopqr stuvwxyz
123456789 0.,;:''&!?$

Pasquale Book 42 point

PANOSE abegmoqst

Pasquale Light 24 point

PANOSE abegmoqst

Pasquale Light Italic 24 point

PANOSE abegmoqst

Pasquale Book Italic 24 point

PANOSE abegmoqst

Pasquale Medium 24 point

PANOSE abegmoqst

Pasquale Medium Italic 24 point

PANOSE abegmoqst

Pasquale Bold 24 point

PANOSE abegmoqst

Pasquale Bold Italic 24 point

Supplier	Compugraphic 8400 Digital Typesetter
Usage	Text, Display
Similar Fonts	
Available Media	
Photo, Digital	
Alternate Names	

	1	2	3	4	5	6	7	8	9	0
serif	X	79	•	X	153	166	X	X	X	X
proportion	93	99	•	X	126	X				
contrast	113	•	X	124	X	X				
arm style	X	X	•	X	123	X	X	X	X	
form	•	X	X	X	X	X				
midline	•	X	X	X	X	X	X	X		
x height	X	•	118	X						

ABCDEF
GHIJKLM
NOPQRS
TUVWXY
abcdefghi
jklmnopq
rstuvwxy
12345678
90.,;''&!?$

ITC Bookman Medium 48 point

PANOSE abegmoqst

ITC Bookman Light 24 point

PANOSE abegmoqst

ITC Bookman Light Italic 24 point

PANOSE abegmoqs

ITC Bookman Medium Italic 24 point

PANOSE abegmoqst

ITC Bookman Demi 24 point

PANOSE abegmoqs

ITC Bookman Demi Italic 24 point

PANOSE abegmo

ITC Bookman Bold 24 point

PANOSE abegmo

ITC Bookman Bold Italic 24 point

Supplier	**Alphatype CRS Digital Typesetter**
Usage	**Text, Display**
Similar Fonts	
Available Media	
Digital, Photo, Hot, Bit, DT, PS	
Alternate Names	
Revival 711(BS), Bookman Oldstyle, Boldface(HC), Bookface, BM(Itek)	

	1	2	3	4	5	6	7	8	9	0
serif	X	79	•	X	153	166	X	X	X	X
proportion	(94)	(102)	•	X	126	X				
contrast	(113)	•	X	124	X	X				
arm style	X	X	•	X	123	X	X	X	X	
form	•	X	X	X	X	X				
midline	•	(122)	X	X	X	X	X	X		
x height	X	(116)	•	X						

ABCDEF GHIJKLM NOPQRST UVWXYZ abcdefghij klmnopqr stuvwxyz 123456789 0.,;:"&!?$

Excelsior 48 point

ABCDEFGHIJKLM NOPQRSTUVWXYZ abcdefghijklm nopqrstuvwxyz 1234567890.,;:"&!?$

Excelsior Bold 24 point

PANOSE abegmoqst

Excelsior Italic 24 point

PANOSE abegmoqst

Excelsior Bold Face No. 2 24 point

PANOSEabegmoqst

Excelsior Bold Face No. 2 Italic 24 point

Supplier	Linotype 300 Laser Typesetter	
Usage	Text	
Similar Fonts	Commerce No.1, Opticon	
Available Media		
Hot, Photo, Digital, Bit		
Alternate Names		
News 702(BS), Newstext, News No.14(CG), Excel, Excella(Dymo), Camelot, EX(Itek)		

	1	2	3	4	5	6	7	8	9	0
serif	X	79	•	X	153	166	X	X	X	X
proportion	(94)	(102)	•	X	126	X				
contrast	(113)	•	X	124	X	X				
arm style	X	X	•	X	123	X	X	X	X	
form	•	X	X	X	X	X				
midline	•	(122)	X	X	X	X	X	X		
x height	X	(116)	•	X						

ABCDEFGH IJKLMNOP QRSTUVW XYZ abcdefghijkl mnopqr stuvwxyz 1234567890.,; :''&!?$

Impressum 36 point

ABCDEFGHIJKLMN OPQRSTUVWXYZ abcdefghijklmnopqr stuvwxyz 1234567890.,;:''&!?$

Impressum Italic 23 point

ABCDEFGHIJKLMN OPQRSTUVWXYZ abcdefghijklmnopqrs tuvwxyz 1234567890.,;:''&!?$

Impressum Bold 21 point

PANOSE abegmoqst

Impressum Bold Italic 24 point

Supplier	**Compugraphic 8400 Digital Typesetter**
Usage	**Text, Display**
Similar Fonts	
Available Media	
Photo, Digital	
Alternate Names	

	1	2	3	4	5	6	7	8	9	0
serif	X	79	•	X	153	166	X	X	X	X
proportion	(94)	(102)	•	X	126	X				
contrast	(113)	•	X	124	X	X				
arm style	X	X	•	X	123	X	X	X	X	
form	•	X	X	X	X	X				
midline	•	(122)	X	X	X	X	X	X		
x height	X	(116)	•	X						

ABCDEF
GHIJKLM
NOPQRST
UVWXYZ
abcdefghij
klmnopqrs
tuvwxyz
1234567890
.,;:''&!?$

Ionic 5 38 point

ABCDEFGHIJKLM
NOPQRSTUVWXYZ
abcdefghijklmnopq
rstuvwxyz
1234567890.,;:''&!?$

Ionic 5 Italic 22 point

ABCDEFGHIJKLM
NOPQRSTUVWXYZ
abcdefghijklmnopqr
stuvwxyz
1234567890.,;:''&!?$

Ionic 5 Bold Face No. 2 21 point

Supplier	**Linotronic 202 Digital Typesetter**
Usage	**Text**
Similar Fonts	
Available Media	
Photo, Digital, Bit	
Alternate Names	

News 701(BS), Newstext, Ionic, Corinth(Auto), Doric(Auto, Dymo), Rex, Windsor, Zar(Dymo), News Text Medium(Alpha)

	1	2	3	4	5	6	7	8	9	0
serif	X	79	•	X	153	166	X	X	X	X
proportion	(94)	(102)	•	X	126	X				
contrast	(113)	•	X	124	X	X				
arm style	X	X	•	X	123	X	X	X	X	
form	•	X	X	X	X	X				
midline	•	(122)	X	X	X	X	X	X		
x height	X	(116)	•	X						

ABCDEFG HIJKLMN OP QRSTUVW XYZ abcdefghij klmnopqr stuvwxyz 123456789 0.,:;''&!?$

Craw Clarendon Book 36 point

ABCDEFGHIJKLMN OPQRSTUVWXYZ abcdefghijklmnopqrs tuvwxyz 1234567890.,:;''&!?$

Craw Clarendon Book Condensed 24 point

ABCDEFGHIJKLM NOPQRSTUVWXYZ abcdefghijklmnopqr stuvwxyz 1234567890.,:;''&!?$

Craw Clarendon 20 point

PANOSE abegmoqst

Craw Clarendon Condensed 24 point

Supplier	**Compugraphic 8400 Digital Typesetter**
Usage	**Display**
Similar Fonts	
Available Media	
Hot, Photo, Digital, Bit	
Alternate Names	
Clarendon 701(BS), Clarion(Auto), Clarique(HC), Craw Clarendon(Alpha, CG)	

	1	2	3	4	5	6	7	8	9	0
serif	X	79	•	X	(153)	166	X	X	X	X
proportion	93	(104)	•	X	126	X				
contrast	113	•	X	(124)	X	X				
arm style	X	X	•	X	123	X	X	X	X	
form	•	X	X	X	X	X				
midline	(118)	•	X	X	X	X	X	X		
x height	X	X	•	X						

ABCDEF
GHIJKLM
NOPQRST
UVWXYZ
abcdefghi
jklmnopq
rstuvwxyz
123456789
0.,;:''&!?$

Melior Medium 48 point

PANOSE abegmoqst

Melior 24 point

PANOSE abegmoqst

Melior Italic 24 point

PANOSE abegmoqst

Melior Medium Italic 24 point

PANOSE abegmoqst

Melior Bold 24 point

PANOSE abegmoqst

Melior Bold Italic 24 point

PANOSE abegmoqst

Melior Black 24 point

PANOSE abegmoqst

Melior Black Italic 24 point

Supplier	**Linotronic 300 Laser Typesetter**
Usage	**Text, Display**
Similar Fonts	**Vermillion, Metrion**
Available Media	
Photo, Digital, DT, Hot, Bit, PS	
Alternate Names	
Zapf Elliptical 711(BS), Melliza(CG), Ballardvale(Auto, Dymo), Lyra, Medallion(HC), Hanover(AM), ME(Itek), Melier, Uranus(Alpha), Ventura(Wang)	

	1	2	3	4	5	6	7	8	9	0
serif	X	80	•	X	X	X	X	X	231	X
proportion	X	X	•	X	X	X				
contrast	X	•	X	X	X	X				
arm style	X	X	116	X	•	X	X	X	X	
form	X	•	X	X	X	X				
midline	X	X	X	X	•	X	X	X		
x height	X	•	X	X						

ABCDEFG
HIJKLMN
OP
QRSTUV
WXYZ
abcdefghij
klmnopqr
stuvwxyz
1234567890.,
:;''&!?$

Claire News Light 36 point

ABCDEFGHIJ
KLMNOPQRST
UVWXYZ
abcdefghijklmn
opqrstuvwxyz
1234567890.,;:'
'&!?$

Claire News Bold 24 point

Supplier	**Compugraphic 8400 Digital Typesetter**
Usage	**Display**
Similar Fonts	
Available Media	
Photo, Digital	
Alternate Names	

	1	2	3	4	5	6	7	8	9	0
serif	57	X	●	X	X	X	X	X	X	X
proportion	X	X	●	X	X	X				
contrast	113	122	X	●	X	X				
arm style	X	X	●	X	X	X	X	X	X	
form	●	X	X	X	X	X				
midline	X	●	X	X	X	X	X	X		
x height	X	X	●	X						

ABCDEF GHIJKLM NOPQRS TUVWXY abcdefghi jklmnopq rstuvwxy 1234567 890.,;"&!?

Helserif Regular 48 point

ABCDEFGHIJKLMN
OPQRSTUVWXYZ
abcdefghijklmnopq
rstuvwxyz
1234567890.,;"&!?$

Helserif Light 24 point

*ABCDEFGHIJKLMN
OPQRSTUVWXYZ
abcdefghijklmnopq
rstuvwxyz
1234567890.,;"&!?$*

Helserif Light Italic 24 point

PANOSE abegmoq

Helserif Medium 24 point

Supplier	**Alphatype CRS Digital Typesetter**
Usage	**Display, Text**
Similar Fonts	
Available Media	
Photo, Digital	
Alternate Names	

	1	2	3	4	5	6	7	8	9	0
serif	X	83	•	X	X	X	(194)	X	X	X
proportion	96	X	•	X	X	X				
contrast	X	X	X	X	X	•				
arm style	X	X	X	X	X	X	•	X	X	
form	•	X	X	X	X	X				
midline	•	X	X	X	X	X	X	X		
x height	X	X	•	X						

ABCDEFG
HIJKLMNO
PQRSTUV
WXYZ abcd
efghijklmno
pqrstuvwx
yz 123456
7890.,;"&!?

ITC Cushing Medium 48 point

PANOSE abegmoqst

ITC Cushing Book 24 point

PANOSE abegmoqst

ITC Cushing Book Italic 24 point

PANOSE abegmoqst

ITC Cushing Medium Italic 24 point

PANOSE abegmoqst

ITC Cushing Bold 24 point

PANOSE abegmoqst

ITC Cushing Bold Italic 24 point

PANOSE abegmoqst

ITC Cushing Heavy 24 point

PANOSE abegmoqst

ITC Cushing Heavy Italic 24 point

Supplier	Alphatype CRS Digital Typesetter
Usage	Text, Display
Similar Fonts	New House
Available Media	
Photo, Digital, Bit, DT	
Alternate Names	
Revival 721(BS)	

	1	2	3	4	5	6	7	8	9	0
serif	X	X	•	X	157	X	198	X	235	X
proportion	93	99	116	X	•	X				
contrast	X	•	127	X	X	X				
arm style	X	X	•	X	X	X	X	X	X	
form	•	X	X	X	X	X				
midline	•	X	X	X	X	X	X	X		
x height	X	•	X	X						

ABCDEFGHIJ KLMNOPQRS TUVWXYZ abcdefghijklm nopqrstuvwxy 1234567890 .,;'"&!?$

iTC Cheltenham Book Condensed 48 point

PANOSE abegmoqst

ITC Cheltenham Light Condensed 24 point

PANOSE abegmoqst

ITC Cheltenham Light Condensed Italic 24 point

PANOSE abegmoqst

ITC Cheltenham Book Condensed Italic 24 point

PANOSE abegmoqst

ITC Cheltenham Bold Condensed 24 point

PANOSE abegmoqst

ITC Cheltenham Bold Condensed Italic 24 point

PANOSE abegmoqst

ITC Cheltenham Ultra Condensed 24 point

PANOSE abegmoqst

ITC Cheltenham Ultra Condensed Italic 24 point

Supplier	**Alphatype CRS Digital Typesetter**
Usage	**Display, Text**
Similar Fonts	**Contact**
Available Media	
Digital, Photo, Bit	
Alternate Names	
Stubserif 705(BS), Cheltonian(HC), Gloucester, Nordhoff(Auto), Winchester	

	1	2	3	4	5	6	7	8	9	0
serif	X	X	•	X	X	X	X	X	X	X
proportion	95	(108)	X	X	•	X				
contrast	X	126	•	X	X	X				
arm style	X	X	•	X	X	X	X	X	X	
form	•	X	X	X	X	X				
midline	•	X	X	X	X	X	X	X		
x height	X	X	•	X						

ABCDEFG
HIJKLMNO
PQRSTUV
WXYZ
abcdefghij
klmnopqr
stuvwxyz
12345678
90.,;:"&!?$

Renault Light Positive 48 point

ABCDEFGHIJKLMNO
PQRSTUVWXYZ
abcdefghijklmnopqrs
tuvwxyz
1234567890.,;:"&!?$

Renault Light Italic Positive 24 point

ABCDEFGHIJKLMN
OPQRSTUVWXYZ
abcdefghijklmnop
qrstuvwxyz
1234567890.,;:"&!?$

Renault Bold Positive 24 point

Supplier	Linotronic 202 Digital Typesetter
Usage	Display, Text
Similar Fonts	Aachen (bold)
Available Media	
Hot, Photo, Digital	
Alternate Names	

	1	2	3	4	5	6	7	8	9	0
serif	63	X	•	X	X	X	X	X	X	X
proportion	X	X	X	X	•	X				
contrast	X	X	X	•	X	X				
arm style	X	X	X	X	•	X	X	X	X	
form	X	•	X	X	X	X				
midline	•	X	X	X	X	X	X	X		
x height	X	•	X	X						

ABCDEFG HIJKLMN OPQRST UVWXYZ abcdefghij klmnopqrst uvwxyz 12345678 90.,;:''&!?$

Trajanus 48 point

ABCDEFGHIJKLMNO
PQRSTUVWXYZ
abcdefghijklmnopqrst
uvwxyz
1234567890.,;:''&!?$

Trajanus Italic 24 point

PANOSE abegmoqst

Trajanus Bold 24 point

PANOSE abegmoqst

Trajanus Bold Italic 24 point

PANOSE abegmoqst

Trajanus Black 24 point

PANOSE abegmoqst

Trajanus Black Italic 24 point

Supplier	**Linotronic 300 Laser Typesetter**
Usage	**Display, Text**
Similar Fonts	**Athenaeum**
Available Media	
Hot, Photo, Digital	
Alternate Names	

	1	2	3	4	5	6	7	8	9	0
serif	**4**	66	90	●	X	160	X	X	X	X
proportion	●	X	(142)	X	X	X				
contrast	X	●	X	X	X	X				
arm style	●	X	X	X	X	X	X	X	X	
form	●	X	X	X	X	X				
midline	●	X	X	X	X	X	X	X		
x height	●	X	X	X						

ABCDEFG
HIJKLMNO
PQRSTUV
WXYZ abcd
efghijklmno
qrstuvwxy
1234567
890.,;"&!?$

ITC Berkeley Old Style Medium 42 point

PANOSE abegmoqst

ITC Berkeley Old Style Book 24 point

PANOSE abegmoqst

ITC Berkeley Old Style Book Italic 24 point

PANOSE abegmoqst

ITC Berkeley Old Style Medium Italic 24 point

PANOSE abegmoqst

ITC Berkeley Old Style Black 24 point

PANOSE abegmoqst

ITC Berkeley Old Style Black Italic 24 point

PANOSE abegmoqst

ITC Berkeley Old Style Bold 24 point

PANOSE abegmoqst

ITC Berkeley Old Style Bold Italic 24 point

Supplier	**Alphatype CRS Digital Typesetter**
Usage	**Text, Display**
Similar Fonts	
Available Media	
Photo, Digital, DT	
Alternate Names	

	1	2	3	4	5	6	7	8	9	0
serif	(15)	66	91	●	X	160	X	X	X	X
proportion	●	X	142	X	X	X				
contrast	X	●	X	X	X	X				
arm style	●	X	X	X	X	X	X	X	X	
form	●	X	X	X	X	X				
midline	X	X	●	X	X	X	X	X		
x height	X	●	X	X						

ABCDEFGH IJKLMNOP QRSTUVWX YZ abcdefghijklm nopqr stuvwxyz 1234567890.,;: '&!?$

Elante 36 point

ABCDEFGHIJKLMN OPQRSTUVWXYZ abcdefghijklmnopqrstu vwxyz 1234567890.,;:''&!?$

Elante Cursive 23 point

ABCDEFGHIJKLM NOPQRSTUVWXYZ abcdefghijklmnopqrst uvwxyz 1234567890.,;:''&!?$

Elante Bold 22 point

PANOSE abegmoqst

Elante Bold Cursive 24 point

Supplier	**Compugraphic 8400 Digital Typesetter**
Usage	**Text, Display**
Similar Fonts	**Tortino**
Available Media	
Photo, Digital	
Alternate Names	

	1	2	3	4	5	6	7	8	9	0
serif	(31)	X	(95)	•	X	(161)	X	X	X	X
proportion	•	135	143	X	X	X				
contrast	X	X	•	X	X	X				
arm style	X	X	•	X	X	X	X	X	X	
form	•	X	X	X	X	X				
midline	X	•	X	X	X	(132)	X	X		
x height	X	•	X	X						

ABCDEFG
HIJKLMN
OPQRSTU
VWXYZ
abcdefghijkl
mnopqrstuv
wxyz
123456789
0.,;:''&!?$

Electra 44 point

ABCDEFGHIJKLMN
OPQRSTUVWXYZ
abcdefghijklmnopqrstu
vwxyz
1234567890.,;:''&!?$

Electra Cursive 24 point

ABCDEFGHIJKLMN
OPQRSTUVWXYZ
abcdefghijklmnopqrst
uvwxyz
1234567890.,;:''&!?$

Electra Bold 24 point

Supplier	Linotype 202 Digital Typesetter
Usage	Text
Similar Fonts	
Available Media	
Photo, Digital, Hot	
Alternate Names	
Elante(CG), Selectra(Auto)	

	1	2	3	4	5	6	7	8	9	0
serif	31	X	95	●	X	161	X	X	X	X
proportion	●	135	143	X	X	X				
contrast	X	X	●	X	X	X				
arm style	X	X	●	X	X	X	X	X	X	
form	●	X	X	X	X	X				
midline	X	(131)	X	X	X	●	X	X		
x height	X	●	X	X						

ABCDEFG
HIJKLMN
OPQRSTU
VWXYZ

abcdefghijk
lmnopqrst
uvwxyz
123456789
0.,;:"&!?$

Comenius Antiqua 44 point

ABCDEFGHIJKLMN
OPQRSTUVWXYZ
abcdefghijklmnopqrst
uvwxyz
1234567890.,;:"&!?$

Comenius Antiqua Italic 24 point

ABCDEFGHIJKLMNO
PQRSTUVWXYZ
abcdefghijklmnopqrstu
vwxyz
1234567890.,;:"&!?$

Comenius Antiqua 24 point

PANOSE abegmoqst

Comenius Antiqua Bold 24 point

Supplier	Alphatype CRS Digital Typesetter
Usage	**Text, Display**
Similar Fonts	
Available Media	
Photo, Digital	
Alternate Names	

	1	2	3	4	5	6	7	8	9	0
serif	X	X	X	●	X	X	X	X	X	X
proportion	●	137	X	X	X	X				
contrast	X	X	X	●	X	X				
arm style	X	X	X	X	●	X	X	X	X	
form	X	●	X	X	X	X				
midline	●	X	X	X	X	X	X	X		
x height	X	●	X	X						

ABCDEFGHI
JKLMNOP
QRSTUVWX
YZ
abcdefghijkl
mnopqr
stuvwxyz
1234567890.
,;:''&!?$

Claridge 36 point

ABCDEFGHIJKLMN
OPQRSTUVWXYZ
abcdefghijklmnopqr
stuvwxyz
1234567890.,;:''&!?$

Claridge Italic 23 point

ABCDEFGHIJKLMN
OPQRSTUVWXYZ
abcdefghijklmnopqr
stuvwxyz
1234567890.,;:''&!?$

Claridge Bold 21 point

PANOSE abegmoqst

Claridge Black 24 point

Supplier	**Compugraphic 8400 Digital Typesetter**
Usage	**Text, Display**
Similar Fonts	
Available Media	
Photo, Digital	
Alternate Names	

	1	2	3	4	5	6	7	8	9	0
serif	39	72	(99)	•	X	162	X	X	224	X
proportion	X	•	X	X	X	X				
contrast	X	•	(135)	X	139	X				
arm style	X	X	•	X	X	X	X	X	X	
form	•	X	X	X	X	X				
midline	•	X	X	X	X	X	X	X		
x height	X	•	X	X						

ABCDEFG HIJKLMNO PQRSTUV WXYZ abcd efghijklmno pqrstuvwxy 1234567 890.,;"&!?$

ITC Clearface Regular 48 point

PANOSE abegmoqst

ITC Clearface Regular Italic 24 point

PANOSE abegmoqst

ITC Clearface Bold 24 point

PANOSE abegmoqst

ITC Clearface Bold Italic 24 point

PANOSE abegmoqst

ITC Clearface Heavy 24 point

PANOSE abegmoqst

ITC Clearface Heavy Italic 24 point

PANOSE abegmoqst

ITC Clearface Black 24 point

PANOSE abegmoqst

ITC Clearface Black Italic 24 point

Supplier	Alphatype CRS Digital Typesetter	
Usage	Text, Display	
Similar Fonts		
Available Media		
Digital, DT, Photo, Hot, Bit		
Alternate Names		
Revival 814(BS)		

	1	2	3	4	5	6	7	8	9	0
serif	(41)	(74)	(106)	•	X	164	X	X	X	X
proportion	131	•	143	X	X	X				
contrast	X	(134)	•	X	139	X				
arm style	X	X	•	X	X	X	X	X	X	
form	•	X	X	X	X	X				
midline	•	X	X	X	X	X	X	X		
x height	X	•	X	X						

ABCDEFG HIJKLMN OPQRSTU VWXYZ

abcdefghijk lmnopqrst uvwxyz 123456789 0.,;:"&!?$

Quadriga-Antiqua Medium 48 point

ABCDEFGHIJKLMNO
PQRSTUVWXYZ
abcdefghijklmnopqrstu
vwxyz
1234567890.,;:'"&!?$

Quadriga-Antiqua Italic 24 point

ABCDEFGHIJKLMNO
PQRSTUVWXYZ
abcdefghijklmnopqrstu
vwxyz
1234567890.,;:"&!?$

Quadriga-Antiqua 24 point

PANOSE abegmoqst
Quadriga-Antiqua Bold 24 point

PANOSE abegmoqst
Quadriga-Antiqua Extra Bold 24 point

Supplier	Alphatype CRS Digital Typesetter
Usage	Display, Text
Similar Fonts	
Available Media	
Photo, Digital	
Alternate Names	

	1	2	3	4	5	6	7	8	9	0
serif	(41)	(74)	(106)	●	X	164	X	X	X	X
proportion	131	●	143	X	X	X				
contrast	X	(134)	●	X	139	X				
arm style	X	X	●	X	X	X	X	X	X	
form	●	X	X	X	X	X				
midline	●	X	X	X	X	X	X	X		
x height	X	●	X	X						

ABCDEFG
HIJKLMN
OPQRSTU
VWXYZ
abcdefghij
klmnopqrs
tuvwxyz
12345678
90.,;:''&!?$

Basilia Haas Medium 44 point

PANOSE abegmoqst

Basilia Haas 24 point

PANOSE abegmoqst

Basilia Haas Italic 24 point

PANOSE abegmoqst

Basilia Haas Medium Italic 24 point

PANOSE abegmoqst

Basilia Haas Bold 24 point

PANOSE abegmoqst

Basilia Haas Bold Italic 24 point

PANOSE abegmoqst

Basilia Haas Black 24 point

PANOSE abegmoqst

Basilia Haas Black Italic 24 point

Supplier	Linotype 202 Digital Typesetter
Usage	Text, Display
Similar Fonts	
Available Media	
Digital	
Alternate Names	

	1	2	3	4	5	6	7	8	9	0
serif	51	X	X	●	X	X	178	X	X	X
proportion	133	●	X	X	X	X				
contrast	X	X	X	●	141	X				
arm style	X	X	X	X	●	X	X	X	X	
form	●	X	X	X	X	X				
midline	X	●	X	X	X	X	X	X		
x height	X	●	X	X						

ABCDEF
GHIJKLM
NOPQRST
UVWXYZ
abcdefghi
jklmnopq
rstuvwxyz
12345678
90.,;:'"&!?$

Walbaum 46 point

ABCDEFGHIJKLM
NOPQRSTUVWXYZ
abcdefghijklmnopq
rstuvwxyz
1234567890.,;:'"&!?$

Walbaum Italic 24 point

ABCDEFGHIJKLM
NOPQRSTUVWXYZ
abcdefghijklmnop
qrstuvwxyz
1234567890.,;:'"&!?$

Walbaum Bold 24 point

PANOSE abegmoqst

Walbaum Bold Italic 24 point

Supplier	**Linotronic 300 Laser Typesetter**
Usage	**Display, Text**
Similar Fonts	**Torino, Bauer Classic**
Available Media	
Digital, Photo, Hot	
Alternate Names	

	1	2	3	4	5	6	7	8	9	0
serif	(51)	X	X	●	X	X	178	X	X	X
proportion	133	●	X	X	X	X				
contrast	X	X	X	●	(141)	X				
arm style	X	X	X	X	●	X	X	X	X	
form	●	X	X	X	X	X				
midline	X	●	X	X	X	X	X	X		
x height	X	●	X	X						

ABCDEFG
HIJKLMN
OPQRSTU
VWXYZ
abcdefghijk
lmnopqrstu
vwxyz
1234567890
0.,;:''&!?$

Bauer Bodoni 48 point

PANOSE abegmoqst
Bauer Bodoni Italic 24 point

PANOSE abegmoqst
Bauer Bodoni Bold Condensed 24 point

PANOSE abegmoqst
Bauer Bodoni Black Condensed 24 point

PANOSE abegmoqst
Bauer Bodoni Bold 24 point

PANOSE abegmoqst
Bauer Bodoni Bold Italic 24 point

PANOSEabegmoqst
Bauer Bodoni Extra Bold 24 point

PANOSEabegmoqst
Bauer Bodoni Extra Bold Italic 24 point

Supplier	Linotype 202 Digital Typesetter
Usage	Display, Text
Similar Fonts	Euro Bodoni, Headline Bodoni
Available Media	
Hot, Photo, Bit, Digital	
Alternate Names	
Modern 405(BS), Bodoni	

	1	2	3	4	5	6	7	8	9	0
serif	X	X	X	●	X	X	X	X	X	X
proportion	X	●	X	X	X	X				
contrast	X	134	135	X	●	X				
arm style	X	X	●	X	(141)	X	X	X	X	
form	●	X	X	X	X	X				
midline	X	●	X	X	X	X	X	X		
x height	X	●	X	X						

ABCDEFG
HIJKLMNO
PQRSTUV
WXYZ abcd
efghijklmno
pqrstuvwxy
1234567
890.,;''&!?$

ITC Fenice Regular 48 point

PANOSE abegmoqst

ITC Fenice Light 24 point

PANOSE abegmoqst

ITC Fenice Light Italic 24 point

PANOSE abegmoqst

ITC Fenice Regular Italic 24 point

PANOSE abegmoqst

ITC Fenice Bold 24 point

PANOSE abegmoqst

ITC Fenice Bold Italic 24 point

PANOSE abegmoq

ITC Fenice Ultra 24 point

PANOSE abegmoq

ITC Fenice Ultra Italic 24 point

Supplier	**Alphatype CRS Digital Typesetter**
Usage	**Display, Text**
Similar Fonts	**Corvinus, Firenze**
Available Media	
Photo, Digital, DT, Bit	
Alternate Names	
Industrial 817(BS)	

	1	2	3	4	5	6	7	8	9	0
serif	X	X	X	●	X	X	X	X	X	X
proportion	X	●	X	X	X	X				
contrast	X	X	X	137	●	X				
arm style	X	X	139	X	●	X	X	X	X	
form	●	X	X	X	X	X				
midline	●	X	X	X	X	X	X	X		
x height	X	X	●	X						

ABCDEFGH IJKLMNOP QRSTUVWX YZ abcdefghi jklmnopqrstu vwxyz123456 7890.,;'"&!?$

Bodoni 48 point

PANOSE abegmoqst

Bodoni Book 24 point

PANOSE abegmoqst

Bodoni Book Italic 24 point

PANOSE abegmoqst

Bodoni Italic 24 point

PANOSE abegmoqst

Bodoni Bold 24 point

PANOSE abegmoqst

Bodoni Bold Italic 24 point

PANOSE abegmoqst

Bodoni Extrabold 24 point

PANOSE abegmoqst

Bodoni Extrabold Italic 24 point

Supplier	Alphatype CRS Digital Typesetter
Usage	Display, Text
Similar Fonts	Didi, Manhattan
Available Media	
Digital, Photo, Hot, Ludlow, Bit, PS	
Alternate Names	
Modern 421(BS), Bauer Bodoni, BO(Itek), Brunswick(Wang)	

	1	2	3	4	5	6	7	8	9	0
serif	X	X	X	●	X	X	X	X	X	X
proportion	X	●	X	X	X	X				
contrast	X	X	X	(137)	●	X				
arm style	X	X	(139)	X	●	X	X	X	X	
form	●	X	X	X	X	X				
midline	X	●	X	X	X	X	X	X		
x height	X	●	X	X						

ABCDEFG
HIJKLMN
OPQRSTU
VWXYZ
abcdefghijkl
mnopqrstuv
wxyz
12345678
90.,;:''&!?$

Bernhard Modern 44 point

ABCDEFGHIJKLMN
OPQRSTUVWXYZ
abcdefghijklmnopqrstuv
wxyz
1234567890.,;:''&!?$

Bernhard Modern Italic 24 point

ABCDEFGHIJKLMN
OPQRSTUVWXYZ
abcdefghijklmnopqrst
uvwxyz
1234567890.,;:''&!?$

Bernhard Modern Bold 24 point

PANOSE abegmoqst

Bernhard Modern Bold Italic 24 point

Supplier	Linotype 202 Digital Typesetter
Usage	**Display**
Similar Fonts	Edwards, Metropolis
Available Media	
Photo, Digital, Hot	
Alternate Names	

	1	2	3	4	5	6	7	8	9	0
serif	53	X	X	●	X	X	X	X	X	X
proportion	(129)	X	●	X	X	X				
contrast	X	●	X	X	X	X				
arm style	●	X	X	X	X	X	X	X	X	
form	●	X	X	X	X	X				
midline	●	X	X	X	X	X	X	X		
x height	●	X	X	X						

ABCDEFG HIJKLMN OPQRST UVWXYZ abcdefghi jklmnopq rstuvwxyz 1234567 890.,;'"&!?

ITC Zapf Book Medium 48 point

PANOSE abegmoqst

ITC Zapf Book Light 24 point

PANOSE abegmoqst

ITC Zapf Book Light Italic 24 point

PANOSE abegmoqst

ITC Zapf Book Medium Italic 24 point

PANOSE abegmoq

ITC Zapf Book Demi 24 point

PANOSE abegmoqst

ITC Zapf Book Demi Italic 24 point

PANOSE abegmo

ITC Zapf Book Heavy 24 point

PANOSE abegmoq

ITC Zapf Book Heavy Italic 24 point

Supplier	Alphatype CRS Digital Typesetter
Usage	Text, Display
Similar Fonts	Craw Modern
Available Media	
Digital, Photo, Bit	
Alternate Names	
Elliptical 716(BS), ZF(Itek)	

	1	2	3	4	5	6	7	8	9	0
serif	56	X	X	●	X	167	X	X	X	X
proportion	131	135	●	X	X	X				
contrast	X	X	●	X	X	X				
arm style	X	X	●	X	X	X	X	X	X	
form	X	●	X	X	X	X				
midline	●	X	X	X	X	X	X	X		
x height	X	●	X	X						

ABCDEF GHIJKLM NOPQRST UVWXYZ abcdefghij klmnopqr stuvwxyz 12345678 90.,;:"&!?$

Normande 36 point

ABCDEFGHI JKLMNOPQ RSTUVWXYZ abcdefghijklmn opqrstuvwxyz 1234567890 .,;:"&!?$

Normande Italic 30 point

Supplier	**Linotronic 300 Laser Typesetter**
Usage	**Display**
Similar Fonts	**Thorowgood, Pistilli Roman**
Available Media	
Photo, Digital, Hot	
Alternate Names	

	1	2	3	4	5	6	7	8	9	0
serif	X	X	X	●	X	X	X	X	X	X
proportion	X	X	●	X	X	X				
contrast	X	X	X	X	●	X				
arm style	X	X	X	X	X	X	●	X	X	
form	●	X	X	X	X	X				
midline	●	X	X	X	X	X	X	X		
x height	X	X	●	X						

ABCDEFGH
IJKLMNOP
QRSTUV
WXYZ
abcdefghi
jklmnopqr
stuvwxyz
1234567890
. , ; : ' " & ! ? $

Letter Gothic 48 point

ABCDEFGHIJKL
MNOPQRSTUVWXYZ
abcdefghijklm
nopqrstuvwxyz
1234567890.,;:''&!?

Letter Gothic Italic 24 point

ABCDEFGHIJKL
MNOPQRSTUVWXYZ
abcdefghijklm
nopqrstuvwxyz
1234567890.,;:''&!?

Letter Gothic Bold 24 point

PANOSE abegmoqs

Letter Gothic Bold Italicv

Supplier	Linotype 100 PostScript		
Usage	**Text**		
Similar Fonts			
Available Media			
Photo, Digital, PS, Bit			
Alternate Names			.
Fixed Pitch 850(BS)			

	1	2	3	4	5	6	7	8	9	0
serif	X	X	X	●	X	X	X	X	X	X
proportion	X	X	X	X	X	●				
contrast	X	X	X	X	X	●				
arm style	●	X	X	X	X	X	(147)	X	X	
form	●	X	X	X	X	X				
midline	●	X	X	X	X	X	X	X		
x height	X	X	●	X						

ABCDEFGH
IJKLMNOP
QRSTUV
WXYZ
abcdefghi
jklmnopqr
stuvwxyz
1234567890
.,;:'"&!?$

Courier 48 point

ABCDEFGHIJKL
MNOPQRSTUVWXYZ
abcdefghijklm
nopqrstuvwxyz
1234567890.,;:''&!?

Courier Italic 24 point

ABCDEFGHIJKL
MNOPQRSTUVWXYZ
abcdefghijklm
nopqrstuvwxyz
1234567890.,;:'&!?

Courier Bold 24 point

PANOSE abegmoqst

Courier Bold Italic 24 point

Supplier	**Linotype 100 PostScript**
Usage	**Text**
Similar Fonts	
Available Media	
Hot, Digital, PS, Bit	
Alternate Names	
Fixed Pitch 810(BS)	

	1	2	3	4	5	6	7	8	9	0
serif	X	X	X	•	159	X	X	X	X	X
proportion	X	X	X	X	X	•				
contrast	X	X	X	X	X	•				
arm style	145	X	X	X	X	X	•	X	X	
form	•	X	X	X	X	X				
midline	•	X	X	X	X	X	X	X		
x height	X	•	147	X						

ABCDEFG
HIJKLMN
OPQRSTU
VWXYZ

abcdefghijk
lmnopqrst
uvwxyz
123456789
O.,;:' "&!?$

Typewriter 36 point

ABCDEFGHIJ
KLMNOP
QRSTUVWXYZ
abcdefghij
klmnopqr
stuvwxyz
1234567890
.,;:' '&!?$

Typewriter Large Elite 42 point

Supplier	Alphatype CRS Digital Typesetter
Usage	Text
Similar Fonts	Underwood Typewriter, Remington
Available Media	
Hot, Photo, Digital	
Alternate Names	

	1	2	3	4	5	6	7	8	9	0
serif	X	X	X	●	159	X	X	X	X	X
proportion	X	X	X	X	X	●				
contrast	X	X	X	X	X	●				
arm style	(145)	X	X	X	X	X	●	X	X	
form	●	X	X	X	X	X				
midline	●	(148)	X	X	X	X	X	X		
x height	X	(146)	●	X						

ABCDEFGH
IJKLMNOP
QRSTUV
WXYZ
abcdefghi
jklmnopqr
stuvwxyz
1234567890
. , ; : ' " & ! ? $

Prestige Elite 48 point

ABCDEFGHIJKL
MNOPQRSTUVWXYZ
abcdefghijklm
nopqrstuvwxyz
1234567890 . , ; : ' ' & ! ?

Prestige Elite Oblique 24 point

ABCDEFGHIJKL
MNOPQRSTUVWXYZ
abcdefghijklm
nopqrstuvwxyz
1234567890 . , ; : ' ' & ! ?

Prestige Elite Bold 24 point

PANOSE abegmoqs

Prestige Elite Bold Oblique 24 point

Supplier	**Linotronic 202 Digital Typesetter**
Usage	**Text**
Similar Fonts	**Clarinda Typewriter**
Available Media	
Photo, Digital, Bit, PS	
Alternate Names	
Fixed Pitch 800(BS)	

	1	2	3	4	5	6	7	8	9	0
serif	X	X	X	•	159	X	X	X	X	X
proportion	X	X	X	X	X	•				
contrast	X	X	X	X	X	•				
arm style	145	X	X	X	X	X	•	X	X	
form	•	X	X	X	X	X				
midline	147	•	X	X	X	X	X	X		
x height	X	X	•	X						

ABCDEFGHIJ
KLMNOP
QRSTUVWX
YZ
abcdefghijklm
nopqr
stuvwxyz
1234567890.,;:
''&!?$

Schneidler Light 36 point

ABCDEFGHIJKLMNO
PQRSTUVWXYZ
abcdefghijklmnopqrstuvw
xyz
1234567890.,;:''&!?$

Schneidler Light Italic 24 point

PANOSE abegmoqst

Schneidler Bold 24 point

PANOSE abegmoqst

Schneidler Bold Italic 24 point

PANOSE abegmoqst

Schneidler Black 24 point

PANOSE abegmoqst

Schneidler Black Italic 24 point

Supplier	**Compugraphic 8400 Digital Typesetter**
Usage	**Text, Display**
Similar Fonts	**Schneidler Oldstyle**
Available Media	
Photo, Digital	
Alternate Names	

	1	2	3	4	5	6	7	8	9	0
serif	X	X	X	X	●	X	X	X	216	X
proportion	●	X	152	X	X	X				
contrast	●	X	X	X	X	X				
arm style	●	X	X	X	X	X	X	X	X	
form	●	X	X	X	X	X				
midline	X	X	X	X	X	●	X	X		
x height	X	●	X	X						

ABCDEF GHIJKLM NOPQRS TUVW XYZ abcdefghij klmnopqrs tuvwxyz 123456789 0.,;:''&!?$

Worchester Round Medium 48 point

ABCDEFGHIJKLMN
OPQRSTUVWXYZ
abcdefghijklmnopqrstuv
wxyz
1234567890.,;:''&!?$

Worchester Round 24 point

*ABCDEFGHIJKLMNO
PQRSTUVWXYZ
abcdefghijklmnop
qrstuvwxyz
1234567890.,;:''&!?$*

Worchester Round Italic 24 point

PANOSE abegmoqst

Worchester Round Bold 24 point

Supplier	**Linotronic 202 Digital Typesetter**
Usage	**Text, Display**
Similar Fonts	
Available Media	
Photo, Digital	
Alternate Names	

	1	2	3	4	5	6	7	8	9	0
serif	38	71	X	X	●	X	X	X	X	X
proportion	X	●	X	X	X	X				
contrast	X	●	151	X	X	X				
arm style	●	X	X	X	X	X	X	X	X	
form	●	X	X	X	X	X				
midline	●	X	X	X	X	X	X	X		
x height	X	●	X	X						

ABCDEFG HIJKLMNO PQRSTUV WXYZ abc defghijklm nopqrstuv wxyz 123 4567890 .,;"&!?$

Packer Text Medium 48 point

ABCDEFGHIJKLMNOP QRSTUVWXYZ abcdefghijklmnopqrs tuvwxyz 1234567890.,;"&!?$

Packer Text Medium Italic 24 point

PANOSE abegmoqst

Packer Text Light 24 point

PANOSE abegmoqst

Packer Text Light Italic 24 point

PANOSE abegmoqst

Packer Text Bold 24 point

PANOSE abegmoqst

Packer Text Extrabold 24 point

Supplier	**Alphatype CRS Digital Typesetter**
Usage	**Text, Display**
Similar Fonts	
Available Media	
Photo, Digital	
Alternate Names	

	1	2	3	4	5	6	7	8	9	0
serif	40	X	(105)	X	•	X	X	X	X	X
proportion	X	•	(156)	X	X	X				
contrast	X	150	•	X	X	X				
arm style	•	X	X	X	X	X	X	X	X	
form	•	X	X	X	X	X				
midline	•	X	X	X	X	X	X	X		
x height	X	X	•	X						

ABCDEF
GHIJKLM
NOPQRST
UVWXYZ
abcdefghij
klmnopqr
stuvwxyz
123456789
O.,;:"&!?$

Bryn Mawr Medium 48 point

PANOSE abegmoqst

Bryn Mawr Light 24 point

PANOSE abegmoqst

Bryn Mawr Light Italic 24 point

PANOSE abegmoqst

Bryn Mawr Book 24 point

PANOSE abegmoqst

Bryn Mawr Book Italic 24 point

PANOSE abegmoqst

Bryn Mawr Medium Italic 24 point

PANOSE abegmoqst

Bryn Mawr Bold 24 point

PANOSE abegmoqst

Bryn Mawr Bold Italic 24 point

Supplier	**Linotype 300 Laser Typesetter**
Usage	**Display, Text**
Similar Fonts	
Available Media	
Photo, Digital	
Alternate Names	

	1	2	3	4	5	6	7	8	9	0
serif	52	78	X	X	●	X	X	X	X	X
proportion	149	X	●	X	X	X				
contrast	●	X	156	X	X	X				
arm style	●	X	X	X	X	X	X	X	X	
form	●	X	X	X	X	X				
midline	X	X	●	X	X	X	X	X		
x height	X	●	X	X						

ABCDEF
GHIJKLM
NOPQRS
TUVWXY
abcdefghi
jklmnopq
rstuvwxy
1234567
890.,;"&!?

Scenario Demi 48 point

ABCDEFGHIJKLMNO
PQRSTUVWXYZ
abcdefghijklmnopq
rstuvwxyz
1234567890.,;"&!?$

Scenario Light 24 point

*ABCDEFGHIJKLMNO
PQRSTUVWXYZ
abcdefghijklmnopq
rstuvwxyz
1234567890.,;"&!?$*

Scenario Light Italic 24 point

PANOSE abegmoq

Scenario Bold 24 point

Supplier	Alphatype CRS Digital Typesetter
Usage	Display, Text
Similar Fonts	Skinner
Available Media	
Photo, Digital	
Alternate Names	

	1	2	3	4	5	6	7	8	9	0
serif	X	79	**122**	X	•	166	X	X	X	X
proportion	X	X	•	X	157	X				
contrast	X	•	X	X	X	X				
arm style	X	X	•	X	X	X	X	X	X	
form	•	X	X	X	X	X				
midline	X	•	X	X	X	X	X	X		
x height	X	X	•	X						

ABCDEF GHIJKLM NOPQRS TUVWXY abcdefghij klmnopqr stuvwxy 1234567 890.,;"&!?

ITC Souvenir Medium 48 point

PANOSE abegmoqst

ITC Souvenir Light 24 point

PANOSE abegmoqst

ITC Souvenir Light Italic 24 point

PANOSE abegmoqst

ITC Souvenir Medium Italic 24 point

PANOSE abegmoq

ITC Souvenir Demi 24 point

PANOSE abegmoq

ITC Souvenir Demi Italic 24 point

PANOSE abegmo

ITC Souvenir Bold 24 point

PANOSE abegmo

ITC Souvenir Bold Italic 24 point

Supplier	Alphatype CRS Digital Typesetter
Usage	Display, Text
Similar Fonts	Eastern Souvenir, Holland
Available Media	
Digital, DT, Photo, Bit, PS	
Alternate Names	
Freeform 731(BS), Sovran(Wang), SV(Itek)	

	1	2	3	4	5	6	7	8	9	0
serif	X	79	116	X	•	166	X	X	X	X
proportion	X	X	•	X	157	X				
contrast	X	•	X	X	X	X				
arm style	X	X	•	X	X	X	X	X	X	
form	•	X	X	X	X	X				
midline	X	X	•	X	X	X	X	X		
x height	X	•	X	X						

ABCDEFGH IJKLMNOP QRSTUVW XYZ abcdefghijklm nopqr stuvwxyz 1234567890 .,;:"&!?$

Hadriano Roman 36 point

ABCDEFGHIJKLMN OPQRSTUVWXYZ abcdefghijklmnopqrstu vwxyz 1234567890.,;:"&!?$

Hadriano Light 22 point

ABCDEFGHIJKLMN OPQRSTUVWXYZ abcdefghijklmnopqrst uvwxyz 1234567890.,;:"&!?$

Hadriano Bold 21 point

PANOSE abegmoqst

Hadriano Extra Bold Condensed 24 point

PANOSE abegmoqst

Hadriano Extra Bold 24 point

Supplier	**Compugraphic 8400 Digital Typesetter**
Usage	**Display**
Similar Fonts	
Available Media	
Photo, Digital	
Alternate Names	

	1	2	3	4	5	6	7	8	9	0
serif	X	79	116	X	•	166	X	X	X	X
proportion	X	X	•	X	157	X				
contrast	X	•	X	X	X	X				
arm style	X	X	•	X	X	X	X	X	X	
form	X	•	X	X	X	X				
midline	•	X	X	X	X	X	X	X		
x height	X	•	X	X						

ABCDEFG HIJKLMN OP QRSTUVW XYZ abcdefghij klmno pqr stuvwxyz 1234567890.,;:"&!?$

Cooper Black 36 point

ABCDEFGHIJK LMNOPQRSTU VWXYZ abcdefghijklm nopqrstuvwxyz 1234567890.,;:" &!?$

Cooper Black Italic 27 point

Supplier	Compugraphic 8400 Digital Typesetter
Usage	Display
Similar Fonts	Pabst
Available Media	
Digital, DT, Photo, Hot, Bit, PS	
Alternate Names	
Freeform 741(BS), Pabst(Merg), Pittsburg Black	

	1	2	3	4	5	6	7	8	9	0
serif	54	X	X	X	●	X	X	X	X	X
proportion	X	151	●	X	X	X				
contrast	152	X	●	X	X	X				
arm style	●	X	X	X	X	X	X	X	X	
form	●	X	X	X	X	X				
midline	●	X	X	X	X	X	X	X		
x height	X	X	●	X						

ABCDEFG HIJKLMN OPQRSTU VWXYZ abcdefghi jklmnopq rstuvwxyz 12345678 90.,;:''&!?$

Seagull Medium Roman 48 point

ABCDEFGHIJKLMNOPQ
RSTUVWXYZ
abcdefghijklmnopqrst
uvwxyz
1234567890.,;:''&!?$

Seagull Light Roman 24 point

ABCDEFGHIJKLMNOPQ
RSTUVWXYZ
abcdefghijklmnopqrst
uvwxyz
1234567890.,;:''&!?$

Seagull Bold Roman 23 point

PANOSE abegmoqst

Seagull Black Roman 24 point

Supplier	Linotronic 300 Laser Typesetter
Usage	Display
Similar Fonts	Parsons, Pax
Available Media	
Photo, Digital, DT	
Alternate Names	

	1	2	3	4	5	6	7	8	9	0
serif	X	X	126	X	●	X	198	X	235	X
proportion	X	X	154	X	●	X				
contrast	X	●	X	X	X	X				
arm style	X	X	●	X	X	X	X	X	X	
form	●	X	X	X	X	X				
midline	X	X	●	X	X	X	X	X		
x height	X	X	●	X						

ABCDEFGHI
JKLMNOP
QRSTUVWX
YZ
abcdefghijk
lmnopqr
stuvwxyz
1234567890
.,;:''&!?$

ITC American Typewriter Medium Condensed 48 point

ABCDEFGHIJKLMNOPQR
STUVWXYZ
abcdefghijklmnopqrstuvw
xyz
1234567890.,;:''&!?$

ITC American Typewriter Light Condensed 24 point

ABCDEFGHIJKLMNOP
QRSTUVWXYZ
abcdefghijklmnopqrstu
vwxyz
1234567890.,;:''&!?$

ITC American Typewriter Bold Condensed 24 point

Supplier	**Compugraphic 8400 Digital Typesetter**
Usage	**Display, Text**
Similar Fonts	
Available Media	
Photo, Digital, Bit, DT	
Alternate Names	
Typewriter 911(BS)	

	1	2	3	4	5	6	7	8	9	0
serif	X	87	X	X	•	X	209	X	X	X
proportion	X	X	X	X	•	159				
contrast	X	X	X	X	X	•				
arm style	X	X	X	X	X	X	•	X	X	
form	•	X	X	X	X	X				
midline	X	•	X	X	X	X	X	X		
x height	X	X	•	X						

ABCDEFG HIJKLM NOPQRST UVWXYZ abcdefghij klmnopqr stuvwxyz 1234567 890.,;''&!?

ITC American Typewriter Medium 48 point

ABCDEFGHIJKLMN
OPQRSTUVWXYZ
abcdefghijklmnopqr
stuvwxyz
1234567890.,;:''&!?$

ITC American Typewriter Light 24 point

**ABCDEFGHIJKLMN
OPQRSTUVWXYZ
abcdefghijklmnopqr
stuvwxyz
1234567890.,;:''&!?$**

ITC American Typewriter Bold 22 point

Supplier	**Alphatype CRS Digital Typesetter**
Usage	**Text, Display**
Similar Fonts	
Available Media	
Digital, DT, Photo, Bit, PS	
Alternate Names	
Typewriter 911(BS)	

	1	2	3	4	5	6	7	8	9	0
serif	X	X	X	(148)	•	X	X	X	X	X
proportion	X	X	X	X	(158)	•				
contrast	X	X	X	X	X	•				
arm style	X	X	X	X	X	X	•	X	X	
form	•	X	X	X	X	X				
midline	X	•	X	X	X	X	X	X		
x height	X	X	•	X						

ABCDEFGHI
JKLMNOP
QRSTUVWX
YZ
abcdefghijkl
mnopqr
stuvwxyz
1234567890.,
;:''&!?$

Trump Medieval 36 point

ABCDEFGHIJKLMN
OPQRSTUVWXYZ
abcdefghijklmnopqr
stuvwxyz
1234567890.,;:''&)!?$

Trump Medieval Italic 23 point

ABCDEFGHIJKLMN
OPQRSTUVWXYZ
abcdefghijklmnopqrs
tuvwxyz
1234567890.,;:''&!?$

Trump Medieval Bold 23 point

PANOSE abegmoqst

Trump Medieval Bold Italic 24 point

Supplier	Compugraphic 8400 Digital Typesetter
Usage	Text, Display
Similar Fonts	
Available Media	
Digtial, Photo, Hot, DT, PS	
Alternate Names	
Continental(HC), Knight(Wang), Mediaeval(AM), Olympus(Alpha), Saul(Auto), Trump Imperial	

	1	2	3	4	5	6	7	8	9	0
serif	(51)	(66)	(90)	129	X	●	X	X	X	X
proportion	●	X	X	X	X	X				
contrast	X	●	X	X	X	X				
arm style	●	X	X	X	X	X	X	X	X	
form	●	X	X	X	X	X				
midline	●	X	X	X	X	X	X	X		
x height	X	●	X	X						

ABCDEFG HIJKLMN OPQRSTU VWXYZ abcdefghij klmnopqrs tuvwxyz 1234567 890.,;"&!?$

ITC Veljovic Medium 48 point

PANOSE abegmoqst

ITC Veljovic Book 24 point

PANOSE abegmoqst

ITC Veljovic Book Italic 24 point

PANOSE abegmoqst

ITC Veljovic Medium Italic 24 point

PANOSE abegmoqst

ITC Veljovic Bold 24 point

PANOSE abegmoqst

ITC Veljovic Bold Italic 24 point

PANOSE abegmoq

ITC Veljovic Black 24 point

PANOSE abegmoq

ITC Veljovic Black Italic 24 point

Supplier	**Alphatype CRS Digital Typesetter**
Usage	**Text, Display**
Similar Fonts	**Mediaeval, Augustea Nova**
Available Media	
Photo, Digital	
Alternate Names	

	1	2	3	4	5	6	7	8	9	0
serif	(31)	X	(95)	(131)	X	•	X	X	X	X
proportion	•	(164)	167	X	X	X				
contrast	X	X	•	X	X	X				
arm style	X	X	•	X	X	X	X	X	X	
form	•	X	X	X	X	X				
midline	X	•	X	X	X	X	X	X		
x height	X	•	X	X						

ABCDEFGHI JKLMNOP QRSTUVWX YZ
abcdefghijkl mnopqr stuvwxyz 1234567890. ,;:''&!?$

Maximal Medium 36 point

ABCDEFGHIJKLMN OPQRSTUVWXYZ abcdefghijklmnopqr stuvwxyz 1234567890.,;:''&!?$

Maximal Bold 21 point

PANOSE abegmoqst

Maximal Light 24 point

PANOSE abegmoqst

Maximal Light Italic 24 point

PANOSE abegm oqst

Maximal Extra Bold 24 point

PANOSE abegm oqst

Maximal Black 24 point

Supplier	Compugraphic 8400 Digital Typesetter
Usage	Display, Text
Similar Fonts	
Available Media	
Photo, Digital, Bit	
Alternate Names	
Latine(Auto, Dymo), Zenith(Wang), Meridian, Latin 725(BS), Meridien(Merg)	

	1	2	3	4	5	6	7	8	9	0
serif	39	72	**102**	134	X	•	X	X	224	X
proportion	X	•	166	X	X	X				
contrast	X	•	164	X	X	X				
arm style	X	X	•	X	X	X	X	X	X	
form	•	X	X	X	X	X				
midline	•	X	X	X	X	X	X	X		
x height	X	X	•	X						

ABCDEF
GHIJKLM
NOPQRST
UVWXYZ
abcdefghij
klmnopqr
stuvwxyz
123456789
0.,;:"&!?$

Versailles 55 42 point

PANOSE abegmoqst

Versailles Light 45 24 point

PANOSE abegmoqst

Versailles Light Italic 46 24 point

PANOSE abegmoqst

Versailles Italic 56 24 point

PANOSE abegmoqst

Versailles Bold 75 24 point

PANOSE abegmoqst

Versailles Bold Italic 76 24 point

PANOSEabegmoqst

Versailles Black 95 24 point

PANOSE abegmoqst

Versailles Black Italic 96 24 point

Supplier	Linotronic 300 Laser Typesetter
Usage	Text, Display
Similar Fonts	
Available Media	
Photo, Digital	
Alternate Names	

	1	2	3	4	5	6	7	8	9	0
serif	39	72	103	134	X	•	X	X	224	X
proportion	X	•	166	X	X	X				
contrast	X	•	164	X	X	X				
arm style	X	X	•	X	X	X	X	X	X	
form	•	X	X	X	X	X				
midline	X	•	X	X	X	X	X	X		
x height	X	•	X	X						

ABCDEFGHIJ
KLMNOP
QRSTUVWXY
Z
abcdefghijkl
mnopqr
stuvwxyz
1234567890.,
;:'"&!?$

ITC Gamma Medium 36 point

PANOSE abegmoqst

ITC Gamma Book 24 point

PANOSE abegmoqst

ITC Gamma Book Italic 24 point

PANOSE abegmoqst

ITC Gamma Medium Italic 24 point

PANOSE abegmoqst

ITC Gamma Bold 24 point

PANOSE abegmoqst

ITC Gamma Bold Italic 24 point

PANOSE abegmoqst

ITC Gamma Black 24 point

PANOSE abegmoqst

ITC Gamma Black Italic 24 point

Supplier	**Compugraphic 8400 Digital Typesetter**
Usage	**Text, Display**
Similar Fonts	
Available Media	
Photo, Digital	
Alternate Names	
Square 721(BS), Eurogothic(Alpha), Europa(Wang), Microstyle(CG), Aldostyle, ES(Itek), Waltham(Dymo)	

	1	2	3	4	5	6	7	8	9	0
serif	(44)	74	(109)	135	X	•	X	X	X	X
proportion	(161)	•	167	X	X	X				
contrast	X	(163)	•	X	X	X				
arm style	X	X	•	X	X	X	X	X	X	
form	•	X	X	X	X	X				
midline	X	•	X	X	X	X	X	X		
x height	X	•	X	X						

ABCDEFG HIJKLMN OPQRSTU VWXYZ ab cdefghijkl mnopqrs tuvwxyz 1234567 890.,;'"&?!?

ITC Barcelona Medium 48 point

PANOSE abegmoqst

ITC Barcelona Book 24 point

PANOSE abegmoqst

ITC Barcelona Book Italic 24 point

PANOSE abegmoqst

ITC Barcelona Medium Italic 24 point

PANOSE abegmoqst

ITC Barcelona Bold 24 point

PANOSE abegmoqst

ITC Barcelona Bold Italic 24 point

PANOSE abegmoqst

ITC Barcelona Heavy 24 point

PANOSE abegmoqst

ITC Barcelona Heavy Italic 24 point

Supplier	Alphatype CRS Digital Typesetter
Usage	Display, Text
Similar Fonts	Metropolis, Lorena
Available Media	
Photo, Digital, DT	
Alternate Names	

	1	2	3	4	5	6	7	8	9	0
serif	X	X	(113)	X	X	•	X	X	(230)	X
proportion	X	X	•	X	X	X				
contrast	•	166	167	X	X	X				
arm style	X	X	•	X	X	X	X	X	X	
form	•	X	X	X	X	X				
midline	•	X	X	X	X	X	X	X		
x height	X	X	•	X						

ABCDEFG
HIJKLMN
OP
QRSTUVW
XYZ
abcdefghijk
lmnopqr
stuvwxyz
1234567890
.,;:''&!?$

ITC LSC Book Regular 36 point

ABCDEFGHIJKLMN
OPQRSTUVWXYZ
abcdefghijklmnopqrstu
vwxyz
1234567890.,;:''&!?$

ITC LSC Book Regular Italic 19 point

PANOSE abegmoqst

ITC LSC Book Bold 24 point

PANOSE abegmoqst

ITC LSC Book Bold Italic 24 point

PANOSE abegmoqs

ITC LSC Book Extrabold 24 point

PANOSE abegmoqst

ITC LSC Book Extrabold Italic 24 point

Supplier	**Compugraphic 8400 Digital Typesetter**
Usage	**Text, Display**
Similar Fonts	
Available Media	
Photo, Digital, DT	
Alternate Names	

	1	2	3	4	5	6	7	8	9	0
serif	X	79	116	X	153	•	X	X	X	X
proportion	X	162	•	X	X	X				
contrast	165	•	167	X	X	X				
arm style	X	X	•	X	X	X	X	X	X	
form	•	X	X	X	X	X				
midline	•	X	X	X	X	X	X	X		
x height	X	•	X	X						

ABCDEFG HIJKLMN OPQRSTU VWXYZ abcdefghij klmnopqr stuvwxyz 12345678 90.,;:''&!?$

Meridien Medium 44 point

ABCDEFGHIJKLMNO PQRSTUVWXYZ abcdefghijklmnopqrstu vwxyz 1234567890.,;:''&!?$

Meridien Medium Italic 24 point

PANOSE abegmoqst

Meridien 24 point

PANOSE abegmoqst

Meridien Italic 24 point

PANOSE abegmoqst

Meridien Bold 24 point

PANOSE abegmoqst

Meridien Bold Italic 24 point

Supplier	Linotronic 202 Digital Typesetter
Usage	Text, Display
Similar Fonts	Largo
Available Media	
Photo, Digital, Bit	
Alternate Names	
Latine(Auto, Dymo), Zenith(Wang), Meridian, Latin 725(BS)	

	1	2	3	4	5	6	7	8	9	0
serif	56	X	X	143	X	●	X	X	X	X
proportion	161	164	●	X	X	X				
contrast	165	166	●	X	X	X				
arm style	X	X	●	X	X	X	X	X	X	
form	●	X	X	X	X	X				
midline	X	●	X	X	X	X	X	X		
x height	X	X	●	X						

ABCDEFGH
IJKLMNOP
QRSTUVWX
YZ
abcdefghijkl
MNOPQR
STUVWXYZ
12345678
90.,;:"&!?$

Peignot Demi 48 point

ABCDEFGHIJKLMNOP
QRSTUVWXYZ
abcdefghijklmnopqrstuvw
xyz
1234567890.,;:"&!?$

Peignot Light 24 point

ABCDEFGHIJKLMNO
PQRSTUVWXYZ
abcdefghijklmnopqrstu
vwxyz
1234567890.,;:"&!?$

Peignot Bold 24 point

Supplier	**Compugraphic 8400 Digital Typesetter**
Usage	**Display**
Similar Fonts	
Available Media	
Digital, DT, Photo, Hot, Bit	
Alternate Names	
Penyoe(CG), Exotic 350(BS)	

	1	2	3	4	5	6	7	8	9	0
serif	23	68	93	X	X	X	•	X	219	X
proportion	•	X	X	X	198	X				
contrast	X	•	X	X	X	X				
arm style	X	X	•	X	X	X	X	X	X	
form	•	X	X	X	X	X				
midline	X	•	X	X	X	X	X	X		
x height	X	•	X	X						

ABCDEFG
HIJKLMN
OPQRSTU
VWXYZ ab
cdefghijkl
mnopqrst
uvwxyz
1234567
90.,;''&!?$

ITC Avant Garde Gothic Medium 48 point

PANOSE abegmoqst

ITC Avant Garde Gothic Extra Light 24 point

PANOSE abegmoqst

ITC Avant Garde Gothic Extra Light Oblique 24 point

PANOSE abegmoqst

ITC Avant Garde Gothic Book 24 point

PANOSE abegmoqst

ITC Avant Garde Gothic Book Oblique 24 point

PANOSE abegmoqst

ITC Avant Garde Gothic Medium Oblique 24 point

PANOSE abegmoqst

ITC Avant Garde Gothic Demi 24 point

PANOSE abegmoqst

ITC Avant Garde Gothic Demi Oblique 24 point

PANOSE abegmoqs

ITC Avant Garde Gothic Bold 24 point

PANOSE abegmoqs

ITC Avant Garde Gothic Bold Oblique 24 point

Supplier	Alphatype CRS Digital Typesetter
Usage	Display, Text
Similar Fonts	Haverhill, Neuzeit Sans
Available Media	
Digital, DT, Photo, Bit, PS	
Alternate Names	
Geometric 711(BS), AG(Itek), Suave(Wang), Cadence	

	1	2	3	4	5	6	7	8	9	0
serif	X	X	X	X	X	X	●	X	X	X
proportion	●	179	187	196	199	X				
contrast	X	X	X	X	X	●				
arm style	●	X	X	170	X	X	171	X	X	
form	●	X	X	X	X	X				
midline	●	X	X	X	X	X	X	X		
x height	X	X	●	X						

ABCDEFG HIJKLMNO PQRSTUV WXYZ abc defghijklm nopqrstuv wxyz 1234 567890.,; "&!?$

Martin Gothic Medium 48 point

ABCDEFGHIJKLMNO PQRSTUVWXYZ abcdefghijklmnopq rstuvwxyz 1234567890.,;"&!?$

Martin Gothic Medium Italic 24 point

PANOSE abegmoqst

Martin Gothic Light 24 point

PANOSE abegmoqst

Martin Gothic Light Italic 24 point

PANOSE abegmoqst

Martin Gothic Bold 24 point

PANOSE abegmoqst

Martin Gothic Bold Italic 24 point

Supplier	Alphatype CRS Digital Typesetter
Usage	Display, Text
Similar Fonts	L & C Hairline, Bernhard Gothic
Available Media	
Photo, Digital	
Alternate Names	

	1	2	3	4	5	6	7	8	9	0
serif	37	X	X	X	X	X	•	212	X	236
proportion	•	181	192	X	X	X				
contrast	X	X	X	X	X	•				
arm style	169	X	X	•	X	X	171	X	X	
form	•	X	X	X	X	X				
midline	X	X	X	X	•	X	X	X		
x height	X	X	•	X						

ABCDEFGH
IJKLMNOP
QRSTUVW
XYZ
abcdefghij
klmnopqr
stuvwxyz
123456789
0.,;:''&!?$

Frutiger 55 42 point

PANOSE abegmoqst

Frutiger Light 45 24 point

PANOSE abegmoqst

Frutiger Light Italic 46 24 point

PANOSE abegmoqst

Frutiger Italic 56

PANOSE abegmoqst

Frutiger Bold 65 24 point

PANOSE abegmoqst

Frutiger Bold Italic 66 24 point

PANOSE abegmoqst

Frutiger Black 75 24 point

PANOSE abegmoqst

Frutiger Black Italic 76 24 point

Supplier	**Compugraphic 8400 Digital Typesetter**
Usage	**Display, Text**
Similar Fonts	**Erbar, Johnston Nouveau**
Available Media	
Photo, Digital, DT	
Alternate Names	

	1	2	3	4	5	6	7	8	9	0
serif	X	(69)	(96)	X	X	X	•	214	220	237
proportion	•	184	194	X	(209)	X				
contrast	X	X	X	X	X	•				
arm style	169	X	X	170	X	X	•	X	X	
form	•	X	X	X	X	X				
midline	•	X	X	(174)	X	X	X	X		
x height	X	•	X	X						

ABCDEFG HIJKLMNO PQRSTUV WXYZ abcd efghijklmno pqrstuvwxy 12345678 90.,;"&!?$

Gill Sans 48 point

PANOSE abegmoqst

Gill Sans Light 24 point

PANOSE abegmoqst

Gill Sans Light Italic 24 point

PANOSE *abegmoqst*

Gill Sans Italic 24 point

PANOSE abegmoqst

Gill Sans Bold 24 point

PANOSE abegmoqst

Gill Sans Bold Italic 24 point

PANOSE abegmoq

Gill Sans Extra Bold 24 point

PANOSE abegmo

Gill Sans Ultra Bold 24 point

Supplier	**Alphatype CRS Digital Typesetter**
Usage	**Display, Text**
Similar Fonts	**Charcoal, Adsans**
Available Media	
Digital, DT, Photo, Bit	
Alternate Names	
Humanist 521(BS), Eric, Glib(Alpha), Graphic Gothic(Wang)	

	1	2	3	4	5	6	7	8	9	0
serif	X	(69)	(96)	X	X	X	•	214	220	237
proportion	•	184	194	X	(209)	X				
contrast	X	X	X	X	X	•				
arm style	169	X	X	170	X	X	•	X	X	
form	•	X	X	X	X	X				
midline	•	X	X	(174)	X	X	X	X		
x height	X	•	X	X						

ABCDEFG
HIJKLMNO
PQRSTUV
WXYZ
abcdefghijk
lmnopqrstu
vwxyz
123456789
0.,;:"&!?$

Spartan Medium 48 point

PANOSE abegmoqst

Spartan Light 24 point

PANOSE abegmoqst

Spartan Book 24 point

PANOSE abegmoqst

Spartan Book Italic 24 point

PANOSE abegmoqst

Spartan Bold 24 point

PANOSE abegmoqst

Spartan Heavy 24 point

PANOSE abegmoqst

Spartan Black 24 point

PANOSE abegmoqst

Spartan Black Italic 24 point

PANOSE abegmoqs

Spartan Extra Black 24 point

Supplier	Linotronic 202 Digital Typesetter
Usage	Text, Display
Similar Fonts	Airport
Available Media	
Photo, Digital, Hot, Bit	
Alternate Names	
Geometric 212(BS), Futura(Alpha, BH, CG, HC, Merg), Techno(AM, Auto Dymo), Photura(Auto, Dymo), Future, FU(Itek), Sirius, Tempo, Twenty-Cent., Utica(Wang)	

	1	2	3	4	5	6	7	8	9	0
serif	X	69	96	X	X	X	•	214	220	237
proportion	•	184	194	X	211	X				
contrast	X	X	X	X	X	•				
arm style	169	X	X	170	X	X	•	X	X	
form	•	X	X	X	X	X				
midline	X	X	X	•	X	X	X	X		
x height	•	(174)	X	X						

ABCDEFG HIJKLMNO PQRSTUV WXYZ abcd efghijklmno pqrstuvwxy 1234567 890.,;"&!?$

Futura Medium 48 point

PANOSE abegmoqst
Futura Light 24 point

PANOSE abegmoqst
Futura Light Italic 24 point

PANOSE abegmoqst
Futura Book 24 point

PANOSE abegmoqst
Futura Book Italic 24 point

PANOSE abegmoqst
Futura Medium Italic 24 point

PANOSE abegmoqst
Futura Demibold 24 point

PANOSE abegmoqst
Futura Demibold Italic 24 point

PANOSE abegmoqst
Futura Bold 24 point

PANOSE abegmoqst
Futura Bold Italic 24 point

Supplier	Alphatype CRS Digital Typesetter
Usage	Text, Display
Similar Fonts	Futura Catalogue, Al Fortura
Available Media	
Photo, Digital, Hot, Bit, DT	
Alternate Names	
Geometric 211(BS), FU(Itek), Future, Photura(Auto, Dymo), Sirius, Spartan(Merg), Techno(AM, Auto, Dymo), Tempo, Twenty-Cent., Utica(Wang), Alphatura(Alpha)	

	1	2	3	4	5	6	7	8	9	0
serif	X	69	96	X	X	X	•	214	220	237
proportion	•	184	194	X	(211)	X				
contrast	X	X	X	X	X	•				
arm style	169	X	X	170	X	X	•	X	X	
form	•	X	X	X	X	X				
midline	(171)	X	X	•	X	X	X	X		
x height	(173)	•	X	X						

ABCDEFGHIJ
KLMNOP
QRSTUVWX
YZ
abcdefghijkl
mnopqr
stuvwxyz
123456789
O.,;:''&!?$

ITC Ronda 42 point

ABCDEFGHIJKLMNOP
QRSTUVWXYZ
abcdefghijklmnopqrs
tuvwxyz
1234567890.,;:''&!?$

ITC Ronda Light 24 point

ABCDEFGHIJKLMNOP
QRSTUVWXYZ
abcdefghijklmnopqrs
tuvwxyz
1234567890.,;:''&!?$

ITC Ronda Bold 24 point

Supplier	Compugraphic 8400 Digital Typesetter
Usage	Display
Similar Fonts	Wexford
Available Media	
Photo, Digital, Bit, DT	
Alternate Names	
Geometric 751(BS)	

	1	2	3	4	5	6	7	8	9	0
serif	X	69	96	X	X	X	•	214	220	237
proportion	•	184	194	X	211	X				
contrast	X	X	X	X	X	•				
arm style	169	X	X	170	X	X	•	X	X	
form	•	X	X	X	X	X				
midline	171	X	X	•	X	X	X	X		
x height	173	•	X	X						

ABCDEFG HIJKLMN OPQRSTU VWXYZ abcdefghij klmnopqrs tuvwxyz 1234567 890.,;"&!?

ITC Eras Medium 48 point

ABCDEFGHIJKLM NOPQRSTUVWXYZ abcdefghijklmnop qrstuvwxyz 1234 567890.,;"&!?$

ITC Eras Bold 24 point

PANOSE abegmoqst

ITC Eras Light 24 point

PANOSE abegmoqst

ITC Eras Book 24 point

PANOSE abegmoqst

ITC Eras Demi 24 point

PANOSE abegmo

ITC Eras Ultra 24 point

Supplier	**Alphatype CRS Digital Typesetter**
Usage	**Display**
Similar Fonts	**Advertisers Gothic**
Available Media	
Photo, Digital, DT, Bit	
Alternate Names	
Incised 726(BS)	

	1	2	3	4	5	6	7	8	9	0
serif	X	69	96	X	X	X	•	214	220	237
proportion	•	184	194	X	209	X				
contrast	X	X	X	X	X	•				
arm style	169	X	X	170	X	X	•	X	X	
form	X	•	X	X	X	X				
midline	X	X	X	X	•	X	X	X		
x height	X	X	•	X						

ABCDEFG
HIJKLMN
OPQRSTU
VWXYZ

abcdefghijk
lmnopqrst
uvwxyz
123456789
0.,;:'"&!?$

Imago Medium 44 point

PANOSE abegmoqst
Imago Light 24 point

PANOSE abegmoqst
Imago Light Italic 24 point

PANOSE abegmoqst
Imago Book 24 point

PANOSE abegmoqst
Imago Book Italic 24 point

PANOSE abegmoqst
Imago Medium Italic 24 point

PANOSE abegmoqst
Imago Extrabold 24 point

PANOSE abegmoqst
Imago Extrabold Italic 24 point

Supplier	**Alphatype CRS Digital Typesetter**
Usage	**Display, Text**
Similar Fonts	**Headnocker**
Available Media	
Photo, Digital	
Alternate Names	

	1	2	3	4	5	6	7	8	9	0
serif	X	X	98	X	X	X	●	X	X	X
proportion	X	●	X	X	197	X				
contrast	●	X	X	X	X	X				
arm style	X	X	●	X	X	X	X	X	X	
form	X	●	X	X	X	X				
midline	●	X	X	X	X	X	X	X		
x height	X	X	●	X						

ABCDEF
GHIJKLM
NOPQRST
UVWXYZ
abcdefghij
klmnopqr
stuvwxyz
12345678
90.,;:"&!?$

Brittanic 48 point

ABCDEFGHIJKLM
NOPQRSTUVWXYZ
abcdefghijklm
nopqrstuvwxyz
1234567890.,;:"&!?$

Brittanic Bold 24 point

ABCDEFGHIJKLM
NOPQRSTUVWXYZ
abcdefghijklm
nopqrstuvwxyz
1234567890.,;:"&!?$

Brittanic Bold Italic 18 point

Supplier	**Linotype 300 Laser Typesetter**
Usage	**Text, Display**
Similar Fonts	**Colin, Radiant**
Available Media	
Hot, Photo, Digital	
Alternate Names	
Brittania	

	1	2	3	4	5	6	7	8	9	0
serif	50	X	X	137	X	X	•	X	X	X
proportion	X	•	X	X	X	X				
contrast	X	X	X	•	X	X				
arm style	X	X	X	X	•	X	X	X	X	
form	•	X	X	X	X	X				
midline	•	X	X	X	X	X	X	X		
x height	X	X	•	X						

ABCDEF
GHIJKLM
NOPQRS
TUVWXYZ
abcdefghi
jklmnopqr
stuvwxyz
12345678
90.,;:''&!?$

Uncia 46 point

PANOSE abegmoqst

Uncia Light 24 point

PANOSE abegmoqst

Uncia Light Italic 24 point

PANOSE abegmoqst

Uncia Italic 24 point

PANOSE abegmoqst

Uncia Bold 24 point

PANOSE abegmoqst

Uncia Bold Italic 24 point

PANOSE abegmoqst

Uncia Black 24 point

PANOSE abegmoqst

Uncia Black Italic 24 point

Supplier	**Linotronic 300 Laser Typesetter**
Usage	**Text, Display**
Similar Fonts	
Available Media	
Photo, Digital	
Alternate Names	

	1	2	3	4	5	6	7	8	9	0
serif	X	76	X	X	X	X	●	X	X	X
proportion	(169)	●	(187)	(196)	(199)	X				
contrast	X	X	X	X	X	●				
arm style	●	X	X	181	X	X	184	X	X	
form	●	X	X	X	X	X				
midline	●	X	X	X	X	X	X	X		
x height	X	X	●	X						

ABCDEFG
HIJKLMN
OPQRSTU
VWXYZ
abcdefghij
klmnopqrst
uvwxyz
1234567890
.,;:''&!?$

Video Medium 48 point

PANOSE abegmoqst

Video Light 24 point

PANOSE abegmoqst

Video Light Oblique 24 point

PANOSE abegmoqst

Video Medium Oblique 24 point

PANOSE abegmoqst

Video Bold 24 point

PANOSE abegmoqst

Video Bold Oblique 24 point

PANOSE abegmoqst

Video Black 24 point

PANOSE abegmoqst

Video Black Oblique 24 point

Supplier	Linotronic 202 Digital Typesetter
Usage	Text, Display
Similar Fonts	Akzidenz Grotesque
Available Media	
Photo, Digital	
Alternate Names	

	1	2	3	4	5	6	7	8	9	0
serif	X	76	X	X	X	X	•	X	X	X
proportion	169	•	187	196	199	X				
contrast	X	X	X	X	X	•				
arm style	•	X	X	181	X	X	184	X	X	
form	•	X	X	X	X	X				
midline	•	X	X	X	X	X	X	X		
x height	X	X	•	X						

ABCDEF GHIJKLM NOPQRS TUVWXYZ abcdefghi jklmnopqr stuvwxyz 123456789 0.,;:''&!?$

Monotype Grotesque 215 46 point

ABCDEFGHIJKLMN OPQRSTUVWXYZ abcdefghijklmnopqrs tuvwxyz 1234567890.,;:''&!?$

Monotype Grotesque Italic 215 24 point

PANOSE abegmoqst

Monotype Grotesque Light 126 24 point

PANOSE abegmoqst

Monotype Grotesque Light Italic 126 24 point

PANOSE abegmoqst

Monotype Grotesque Bold 216 24 point

PANOSE abegmoqst

Monotype Grotesque Bold Italic 216 24 point

Supplier	Linotronic 202 Digital Typesetter
Usage	Text, Display
Similar Fonts	Al Bluejack
Available Media	
Photo, Digital	
Alternate Names	

	1	2	3	4	5	6	7	8	9	0
serif	X	X	X	X	X	X	•	X	X	X
proportion	170	•	192	X	X	X				
contrast	X	X	X	X	X	•				
arm style	179	X	X	•	X	X	184	X	X	
form	•	X	X	X	X	X				
midline	•	X	X	X	X	X	X	X		
x height	X	•	X	X						

ABCDEFG
HIJKLMNO
PQRSTUV
WXYZ abcd
efghijklmno
pqrstuvwxy
1234567
890.,;"&!?$

News Gothic 48 point

ABCDEFGHIJKLMNOPQ
RSTUVWXYZ
abcdefghijklmnopqrs
tuvwxyz
1234567890.,;"&!?$

News Gothic Italic 24 point

ABCDEFGHIJKLMNOPQ
RSTUVWXYZ
abcdefghijklmnopqr
stuvwxyz
1234567890.,;"&!?$

News Gothic Bold 24 point

PANOSE abegmoqst

News Gothic Condensed 24 point

PANOSE abegmoqst

News Gothic Bold Condensed 24 point

Supplier	**Alphatype CRS Digital Typesetter**
Usage	**Text , Display**
Similar Fonts	
Available Media	
Digital, DT, Photo, Hot, Bit, PS	
Alternate Names	
Gothic 731(BS), Trade Gothic(Merg), Alpha Gothic (Alpha), Classified News Medium(IBM), Toledo	

	1	2	3	4	5	6	7	8	9	0
serif	X	X	X	X	X	X	•	X	X	X
proportion	170	•	192	X	X	X				
contrast	X	X	X	X	X	•				
arm style	179	X	X	•	X	X	184	X	X	
form	•	X	X	X	X	X				
midline	•	X	X	X	X	X	X	X		
x height	X	•	X	X						

ABCDEFGH
IJKLMNOP
QRSTUVWX
YZ
abcdefghijkl
mnopqr
stuvwxyz
12345678
90.,;:''&!?$

Trade Gothic 42 point

PANOSE abegmoqst

Trade Gothic Light 24 point

PANOSE abegmoqst

Trade Gothic Light Italic 24 point

PANOSE abegmoqst

Trade Gothic Italic 24 point

PANOSE abegmoq
st

Trade Gothic Extended 24 point

PANOSE abegmoqst

Trade Gothic Bold No. 2 24 point

PANOSE abegmoqst

Trade Gothic Bold No. 2 Italic 24 point

PANOSE abegmoq

Trade Gothic Bold Extended 24 point

Supplier	**Compugraphic 8400 Digital Typesetter**
Usage	**Display, Text**
Similar Fonts	**Monotone Gothic, Grotesque 8ans**
Available Media	
Photo, Digital, Hot, Bit	
Alternate Names	
Gothic 731(BS), News Gothic(Alpha, Auto, BH, Dymo, HC, Wang), Toledo, Alpha Gothic(Alpha), News Medium (IBM), Trade(CG)	

	1	2	3	4	5	6	7	8	9	0
serif	X	X	X	X	X	X	•	X	X	X
proportion	170	•	192	X	X	X				
contrast	X	X	X	X	X	•				
arm style	179	X	X	•	X	X	184	X	X	
form	•	X	X	X	X	X				
midline	•	X	X	X	X	X	X	X		
x height	X	•	X	X						

ABCDEFG HIJKLMN OPQRSTU VWXYZ abcdefghij klmnopqrs tuvwxyz 12345678 90.,;:"&!?$

Metromedium No. 2 48 point

ABCDEFGHIJKLMNO PQRSTUVWXYZ abcdefghijklmnopqrstu vwxyz 1234567890.,;:"&!?$

Metromedium No. 2 Italic 24 point

PANOSE abegmoqst

Metrolite No. 2 24 point

PANOSE abegmoqst

Metrolite No. 2 Italic 24 point

PANOSE abegmoqst

Metroblack No. 2 24 point

PANOSE abegmoqst

Metroblack No. 2 Italic 24 point

Supplier	Linotronic 202 Digital Typesetter
Usage	Text, Display
Similar Fonts	Meteor
Available Media	
Photo, Digital, Bit	
Alternate Names	
Chelsea Black(Auto, Dymo), Gothic No.3(CG), Geometric 415(BS)	

	1	2	3	4	5	6	7	8	9	0
serif	X	77	X	X	X	X	•	X	226	X
proportion	171	•	194	X	209	X				
contrast	X	X	X	X	X	•				
arm style	179	X	X	181	X	X	•	X	X	
form	•	X	X	X	X	X				
midline	X	•	X	X	X	X	X	X		
x height	X	•	X	X						

ABCDEFG HIJKLMN OPQRSTU VWXYZ

abcdefghijk lmnopqrst uvwxyz 123456789 0.,;:"^&!?$

Oliver Medium 38 point

ABCDEFGHIJKLMNO
PQRSTUVWXYZ
abcdefghijklmnopqrstu
vwxyz
1234567890.,;:"&!?$

Oliver Medium Italic 18 point

PANOSE abegmoqst

Oliver Light 24 point

PANOSE abegmoqst

Oliver Light Italic 24 point

PANOSE abegmoqst

Oliver Italic 24 point

PANOSE abegmoqst

Oliver Bold 24 point

PANOSE abegmoqst

Oliver Bold Italic 24 point

Supplier	Alphatype CRS Digital Typesetter
Usage	Text, Display
Similar Fonts	Conference
Available Media	
Photo, Digital, DT, Bit	
Alternate Names	
Incised 901(BS), Olive(AM), Oliva, Olivette, Olivette Antique(Wang), Alphavanti(Alpha), Antique Olive(Merg), Olive Antique(CG)	

	1	2	3	4	5	6	7	8	9	0
serif	X	77	X	X	X	X	●	X	226	X
proportion	171	●	194	X	209	X				
contrast	X	X	X	X	X	●				
arm style	179	X	X	181	X	X	●	X	X	
form	X	X	X	X	●	X				
midline	●	X	X	X	X	X	X	X		
x height	X	X	●	X						

ABCDEFGH
IJKLMNOP
QRSTUVW
XYZ abcdef
ghijklmnop
qrstuvwxyz
12345678
90.,;"&!?$

ITC Franklin Gothic Medium 48 point

PANOSE abegmoqst

ITC Franklin Gothic Book 24 point

PANOSE abegmoqst

ITC Franklin Gothic Book Italic 24 point

PANOSE abegmoqst

ITC Franklin Gothic Medium Italic 24 point

PANOSE abegmoqst

ITC Franklin Gothic Demi 24 point

PANOSE abegmoqst

ITC Franklin Gothic Demi Italic 24 point

PANOSE abegmoqst

ITC Franklin Gothic Heavy 24 point

PANOSE abegmoqst

ITC Franklin Gothic Heavy Italic 24 point

Supplier	**Alphatype CRS Digital Typesetter**
Usage	**Display**
Similar Fonts	
Available Media	
Digital, DT, Photo, Hot, Ludlow, Bit, PS	
Alternate Names	
Gothic 744(BS), Franklin(CG), Pittsburg(Wang)	

	1	2	3	4	5	6	7	8	9	0
serif	X	X	X	X	X	X	●	X	X	X
proportion	X	●	X	X	X	X				
contrast	X	X	X	X	X	●				
arm style	(179)	X	X	181	X	X	184	X	X	
form	●	X	X	X	X	X				
midline	●	X	X	X	X	X	X	X		
x height	X	X	●	X						

ABCDEF GHIJKLM NOPQRS TUVWXYZ abcdefghij klmnopqrs tuvwxyz 12345678 90.,;:''&!?$

Helvetica 46 point

PANOSE abegmoqst

Helvetica Thin 24 point

PANOSE abegmoqst

Helvetica Light 24 point

PANOSE abegmoqst

Helvetica Light Italic 24 point

PANOSE abegmoqst

Helvetica Italic 24 point

PANOSE abegmoqst

Helvetica Bold 24 point

PANOSE abegmoqst

Helvetica Bold Italic 24 point

PANOSE abegmoqs

Helvetica Heavy 24 point

PANOSE abegmoq

Helvetica Black 24 point

Supplier	**Linotronic 202 Digital Typesetter**
Usage	**Text, Display**
Similar Fonts	
Available Media	
Photo, Digital, Hot, DT, Bit, PS	
Alternate Names	
Swiss 721(BS), Helios(CG), Triumvirate(CG), Geneva(Wang), Newton(Auto, Dymo), Vega(HC), Megaron(AM), HE(Itek), Corvus, Claro	

	1	2	3	4	5	6	7	8	9	0
serif	X	81	X	X	X	X	•	X	X	X
proportion	(169)	(179)	•	(196)	(199)	X				
contrast	X	X	X	X	X	•				
arm style	•	X	X	192	193	X	(194)	X	X	
form	•	(190)	X	X	X	X				
midline	•	X	X	X	X	X	X	X		
x height	X	X	•	X						

ABCDEFGHI JKLMNOP QRSTUVWX YZ abcdefghijkl mnopqr stuvwxyz 1234567890. ,;:'"&!?$

Folio Medium 36 point

ABCDEFGHIJKLMNOPQRSTU VWXYZ abcdefghijklmnopqrstuvw xyz 1234567890.,;:'"&!?$

Folio Bold Condensed 24 point

PANOSE abegmoqst

Folio Light 24 point

PANOSE abegmoqst

Folio Light Italic 24 point

PANOSE abegmoqst

Folio Bold 24 point

PANOSE abegmoqst

Folio Extra Bold 24 point

Supplier	Compugraphic 8400 Digital Typesetter
Usage	Display, Text
Similar Fonts	Tempo
Available Media	
Digital, DT, Photo, Hot	
Alternate Names	

	1	2	3	4	5	6	7	8	9	0
serif	X	81	X	X	X	X	•	X	X	X
proportion	169	179	•	195	199	X				
contrast	X	X	X	X	X	•				
arm style	•	X	X	192	193	X	194	X	X	
form	•	X	X	X	X	X				
midline	X	X	•	X	X	X	X	X		
x height	X	•	X	X						

ABCDEFGH IJKLMNOP QRSTUVW XYZ abcdef ghijklmnop qrstuvwxyz 1234567 890.,;"&!?$

Univers Medium 55 48 point

PANOSE abegmoqst

Univers Light 45 24 point

PANOSE abegmoqst

Univers Light Italic 46 24 point

PANOSE abegmoqst

Univers Medium Italic 56 24 point

PANOSE abegmoqst

Univers Demibold 65 24 point

PANOSE abegmoqst

Univers Demibold Italic 66 24 point

PANOSE abegmoqst

Univers Bold 75 24 point

PANOSE abegmoqst

Univers Bold Italic 76 24 point

Supplier	Alphatype CRS Digital Typesetter
Usage	Text, Display
Similar Fonts	Venus
Available Media	
Digital, DT, Photo, Hot, Bit	
Alternate Names	
Swiss 742(BS), Galaxy, UN(Itek)	

	1	2	3	4	5	6	7	8	9	0
serif	X	81	X	X	X	X	●	X	X	X
proportion	169	179	●	195	199	X				
contrast	X	X	X	X	X	●				
arm style	●	X	X	192	193	X	194	X	X	
form	X	●	X	(191)	X	X				
midline	●	X	X	X	X	X	X	X		
x height	X	●	(190)	X						

ABCDEFG HIJKLMN OPQRST UVWXYZ abcdefghij klmnopqr stuvwxyz 1234567 890.,;''&!?

Heldustry Medium 48 point

ABCDEFGHIJKLMN OPQRSTUVWXYZ abcdefghijklmnop qrstuvwxyz 1234567890.,;''&!?$

Heldustry Medium Italic 24 point

PANOSE abegmoqst

Heldustry Regular 24 point

PANOSE abegmoqst

Heldustry Regular Italic 24 point

PANOSE abegmoqst

Heldustry Demi-Bold 24 point

PANOSE abegqst

Heldustry Demi-Bold Italic 24 point

Supplier	**Alphatype CRS Digital Typesetter**
Usage	**Text, Display**
Similar Fonts	**Arnholm, Headnocker**
Available Media	
Photo, Digital	
Alternate Names	

	1	2	3	4	5	6	7	8	9	0
serif	X	81	X	X	X	X	•	X	X	X
proportion	169	179	•	195	199	X				
contrast	X	X	X	X	X	•				
arm style	•	X	X	192	193	X	194	X	X	
form	187	•	X	X	X	X				
midline	•	X	X	X	X	X	X	X		
x height	X	189	•	X						

ABCDEFG HIJKLMN OPQRSTU VWXYZ abcdefghij klmnopqrs tuvwxyz 1234567 890.,;"&!?

Eurostile 48 point

ABCDEFGHIJKLMNOPQRSTUV
WXYZ abcdefghijklmnopqrst
uvwxyz 1234567890
.,;"&!?$

Eurostile Condensed 24 point

ABCDEFGHIJKLMNO
PQRSTUVWXYZ
abcdefghijklmnopqrst
uvwxyz
1234567890.,;:"&!?$

Eurostile Extended 20 point

PANOSE abegmoq

Eurostile Bold 24 point

PANOSE abegmoqst

Eurostile Bold Condensed 24 point

PANOSE abeg

Eurostile Bold Extended 24 point

Supplier	**Alphatype CRS Digital Typesetter**
Usage	**Display**
Similar Fonts	**Microgramma, Bolt**
Available Media	
Digital, DT, Photo, Hot, Bit	
Alternate Names	
Square 721(BS), Eurogothic(Alpha), Europa(Wang), Microstyle(CG), Aldostyle, ES(Itek), Waltham(Dymo)		

	1	2	3	4	5	6	7	8	9	0
serif	X	81	X	X	X	X	●	X	X	X
proportion	169	179	●	195	207	X				
contrast	X	X	X	X	X	●				
arm style	●	X	X	192	193	X	194	X	X	
form	X	(189)	X	●	X	X				
midline	●	X	X	X	X	X	X	X		
x height	X	●	X	X						

ABCDEF GHIJKLM NOPQRS TUVWXYZ abcdefghijk lmnopqrstu vwxyz 12345678 90.,;:''&!?$

Akzidenz Grotesk 48 point

ABCDEFGHIJKLMN OPQRSTUVWXYZ abcdefghijklmnopqrstu vwxyz 1234567890.,;:''&!?$

Akzidenz Grotesk Italic 24 point

ABCDEFGHIJKLMNO PQRSTUVWXYZ abcdefghijklmnopqr stuvwxyz 1234567890.,;:''&!?$

Akzidenz Grotesk Bold 24 point

PANOSE abegmoqst

Akzidenz Grotesk Light 24 point

PANOSE abegmoqst

Akzidenz Grotesk Black 24 point

Supplier	Linotype 202 Digital Typesetter
Usage	Display, Text
Similar Fonts	Standard, Berliner Grotesk
Available Media	
Hot, Photo, Digital	
Alternate Names	
Ad Grotesk, Grigat	

	1	2	3	4	5	6	7	8	9	0
serif	X	**82**	X	X	X	X	•	X	232	240
proportion	170	**181**	•	X	X	X				
contrast	X	X	X	X	X	•				
arm style	187	X	X	•	193	X	194	X	X	
form	•	X	X	X	X	X				
midline	•	X	X	X	X	X	X	X		
x height	X	•	X	X						

ABCDEFGHI
JKLMNOP
QRSTUVWX
YZ
abcdefghijkl
mnopqr
stuvwxyz
123456789
0.,;:''&!?$

Hobo Medium 42 point

ABCDEFGHIJKLMNOP
QRSTUVWXYZ
abcdefghijklmnopqrst
uvwxyz
1234567890.,;:''&!?$

Hobo Bold 22 point

ABCDEFGHIJKLMNO
PQRSTUVWXYZ
abcdefghijklmnopqrs
tuvwxyz
1234567890.,;:''&!?$

Hobo Extrabold 22 point

Supplier	Compugraphic 8400 Digital Typesetter
Usage	Display
Similar Fonts	Sparkle
Available Media	
Photo, Digital, PS, Bit, DT	
Alternate Names	
Informal 707(BS), Tramp	

	1	2	3	4	5	6	7	8	9	0
serif	X	X	X	X	X	X	●	X	X	X
proportion	X	X	●	X	X	X				
contrast	X	X	X	X	X	●				
arm style	187	X	X	192	●	X	194	X	X	
form	X	X	X	X	●	X				
midline	X	●	X	X	X	X	X	X		
x height	X	X	●	X						

ABCDEFG HIJKLMN OPQRSTU VWXYZ abcdefghij klmnopqrs tuvwxyz 1234567 890.,;"&!?$

ITC Mixage Medium 48 point

PANOSE abegmoqst

ITC Mixage Book 24 point

PANOSE abegmoqst

ITC Mixage Book Italic 24 point

PANOSE abegmoqst

ITC Mixage Medium Italic 24 point

PANOSE abegmoqst

ITC Mixage Bold 24 point

PANOSE abegmoqst

ITC Mixage Bold Italic 24 point

PANOSE abegmoq

ITC Mixage Black 24 point

PANOSE abegmoq

ITC Mixage Black Italic 24 point

Supplier	**Alphatype CRS Digital Typesetter**
Usage	**Text, Display**
Similar Fonts	**Bridger**
Available Media	
Photo, Digital	
Alternate Names	

	1	2	3	4	5	6	7	8	9	0
serif	X	83	(125)	X	X	X	•	X	X	X
proportion	171	184	•	X	209	X				
contrast	X	X	X	X	X	•				
arm style	(187)	X	X	192	193	X	•	X	X	
form	•	X	X	X	X	X				
midline	•	X	X	X	X	X	X	X		
x height	X	X	•	X						

ABCDEF
GHIJKLM
NOPQRS
TUVWXY
abcdefghi
jklmnopq
rstuvwxy
123456
7890.,;"&

Univers Medium Extended 53 42 point

ABCDEFGHIJKLM
NOPQRSTUVWXYZ
abcdefghijklmnop
qrstuvwxyz 1234
567890.,;"&!?$

Univers Demibold Extended 63 24 point

ABCDEFGHIJKLM
NOPQRSTUVWXYZ
abcdefghijklmno
pqrstuvwxyz 1234
567890.,;"&!?$

Univers Extra Bold Extended 83 24 point

PANOSE abegmoq

Univers Light Extended 43 24 point

PANOSE abegmo

Univers Bold Extended 73 24 point

Supplier	**Alphatype CRS Digital Typesetter**
Usage	**Display**
Similar Fonts	**Announce Grotesque**
Available Media	
Photo, Digital, Hot, DT, Bit	
Alternate Names	
Swiss 742(BS), Galaxy(HC), UN(Itek), Alphavers(Alpha), Aries, Boston(Wang), Versatile(Alpha)	

	1	2	3	4	5	6	7	8	9	0
serif	X	X	X	X	X	X	●	X	X	X
proportion	169	179	187	●	199	X				
contrast	X	X	X	X	X	●				
arm style	●	X	X	X	X	X	X	X	X	
form	●	X	X	X	X	X				
midline	●	X	X	X	X	X	X	X		
x height	X	●	(196)	X						

ABCDEFG
HIJKLMNO
PQRSTUV
WXYZ
abcdefghij
klmnopqrst
uvwxyz
123456789
0.,;:''&!?$

Helvetica Extended 36 point

ABCDEFGHIJKLMNO
PQRSTUVWXYZ
abcdefghijklmnopqrst
uvwxyz
1234567890.,;:''&!?$

Helvetica Light Extended 20 point

ABCDEFGHIJKLMNO
PQRSTUVWXYZ
abcdefghijklmnopqr
stuvwxyz
1234567890.,;:''&!?$

Helvetica Bold Extended 18 point

PANOSE abeg

Helvetica Black Extended 24 point

Supplier	Linotronic 202 Digital Typesetter
Usage	Display
Similar Fonts	
Available Media	
Hot, Photo, Digital, Bit, DT	
Alternate Names	
Swiss 721(BS), Helios(CG), Triumvirate(CG), Geneva(Wang), Newton(Auto, Dymo), Vega(HC), Megaron(AM), HE(Itek), Corvus, Claro	

	1	2	3	4	5	6	7	8	9	0
serif	X	X	X	X	X	X	●	X	X	X
proportion	(169)	(179)	(187)	●	(199)	X				
contrast	X	X	X	X	X	●				
arm style	●	X	X	X	X	X	X	X	X	
form	●	X	X	X	X	X				
midline	●	X	X	X	X	X	X	X		
x height	X	(195)	●	X						

ABCDEFGH IJKLMNOP QRSTUVW XYZ abcdefghij klmnopqr stuvwxyz 12345678 90.,;:''&!?$

Clearface Gothic 65 Medium 48 point

ABCDEFGHIJKLMNOPQ RSTUVWXYZ
abcdefghijklmnopqrstuv wxyz
1234567890.,;:''&!?$

Clearface Gothic 55 24 point

ABCDEFGHIJKLMNOP QRSTUVWXYZ
abcdefghijklmnopqrst uvwxyz
1234567890.,;:''&!?$

Clearface Gothic 75 Bold 23 point

PANOSE abegmoqst

Clearface Gothic 45 Light 24 point

PANOSE abegmoqst

Clearface Gothic 95 Black 24 point

Supplier	Compugraphic 8400 Digital Typesetter
Usage	Display
Similar Fonts	Andgear
Available Media	
Photo, Digital, DT	
Alternate Names	

	1	2	3	4	5	6	7	8	9	0
serif	X	X	X	X	X	X	•	X	X	X
proportion	X	177	X	X	•	X				
contrast	•	198	X	X	X	X				
arm style	X	X	•	X	X	X	X	X	X	
form	•	X	X	X	X	X				
midline	•	X	X	X	X	X	X	X		
x height	X	X	•	X						

ABCDEFGHI JKLMNOP QRSTUVWX YZ abcdefghijkl mnopqr stuvwxyz 1234567890 .,;:''&!?$

Globe Gothic Demi 42 point

ABCDEFGHIJKLMNOP
QRSTUVWXYZ
abcdefghijklmnopqrstu
vwxyz
1234567890.,;:''&!?$

Globe Gothic Light 24 point

ABCDEFGHIJKLMNOP
QRSTUVWXYZ
abcdefghijklmnopqrst
uvwxyz
1234567890.,;:''&!?$

Globe Gothic Bold 23 point

PANOSE abegmoqst

Globe Gothic Ultra 24 point

Supplier	**Compugraphic 8400 Digital Typesetter**
Usage	**Display**
Similar Fonts	**Globe**
Available Media	
Photo, Digital	
Alternate Names	

	1	2	3	4	5	6	7	8	9	0
serif	X	X	126	X	157	X	•	X	235	X
proportion	168	X	X	X	•	X				
contrast	197	•	X	X	X	X				
arm style	X	X	•	X	X	X	X	X	X	
form	•	X	X	X	X	X				
midline	X	X	•	X	X	X	X	X		
x height	X	•	X	X						

ABCDEFGH IJKLMNOP QRSTUVWX YZ abcdefghij klmnopqr stuvwxyz 123456789 O.,;:`'&!?$

ITC Avant Garde Gothic Medium Cond 48 point

ABCDEFGHIJKLMNOPQ
RSTUVWXYZ
abcdefghijklmnopqrst
uvwxyz
1234567890.,;:`'&!?$

ITC Avant Garde Gothic Book Cond 24 point

ABCDEFGHIJKLMNOP
QRSTUVWXYZ
abcdefghijklmnopqrst
uvwxyz
1234567890.,;:`'&!?$

ITC Avant Garde Gothic Demi Cond 24 point

PANOSE abegmoqst

ITC Avant Garde Gothic Bold Cond 24 point

Supplier	Compugraphic 8400 Digital Typesetter
Usage	Display
Similar Fonts	Condensed Sans Serif
Available Media	
Photo, Digital, Bit, DT	
Alternate Names	
Geometric 711(BS), AG(Itek), Suave(Wang), Cadence	

	1	2	3	4	5	6	7	8	9	0
serif	X	86	X	X	X	X	•	X	X	X
proportion	(169)	(179)	(187)	(196)	•	X				
contrast	X	X	X	X	X	•				
arm style	•	X	X	X	X	X	209	X	X	
form	•	X	(205)	(207)	X	X				
midline	•	X	X	X	X	X	X	X		
x height	X	X	•	X						

ABCDEFG
HIJKLMN
OPQRSTU
VWXYZ

abcdefghijk
lmnopqrst
uvwxyz
123456789
0.,;:"&!?$

Franklin Gothic Condensed 48 point

ABCDEFGHIJKLMNO
PQRSTUVWXYZ
abcdefghijklmnopqrstu
vwxyz
1234567890.,;:"&!?$

Franklin Gothic Condensed Italic 24 point

ABCDEFGHIJKLMNO
PQRSTUVWXYZ
abcdefghijklmnopqrstu
vwxyz
1234567890.,;:"&!?$

Franklin Gothic Extra Condensed 24 point

Supplier	Linotype 300 Laser Typesetter
Usage	Display
Similar Fonts	
Available Media	
Hot, Photo, Digital, DT	
Alternate Names	
Gothic 744(BS), Franklin(CG), Pittsburg(Wang)	

	1	2	3	4	5	6	7	8	9	0
serif	X	86	X	X	X	X	•	X	X	X
proportion	(169)	(179)	(187)	(196)	•	X				
contrast	X	X	X	X	X	•				
arm style	•	X	X	X	X	X	209	X	X	
form	•	X	(205)	(207)	X	X				
midline	•	X	X	X	X	X	X	X		
x height	X	X	•	X						

ABCDEFGHI JKLMNOPQ RSTUVW XYZ abcdefghijkl mnopqrstu vwxyz 1234567890 .,:'" &!?$

Helvetica Bold Condensed 48 point

PANOSE abegmoqst
Helvetica Light Condensed 24 point

PANOSE abegmoqst
Helvetica Light Condensed Italic 24 point

PANOSE abegmoqst
Helvetica Condensed 24 point

PANOSE abegmoqst
Helvetica Condensed Italic 24 point

PANOSE abegmoqst
Helvetica Bold Condensed Italic 24 point

PANOSE abegmoqst
Helvetica Black Condensed 24 point

PANOSE abegmoqst
Helvetica Black Condensed Italic 24 point

Supplier	Linotype 100 PostScript
Usage	Display
Similar Fonts	
Available Media	
Digital, Hot, Photo, DT, PS	
Alternate Names	
Swiss 721(BS), Helios(CG), Triumvirate(CG), Geneva(Wang), Newton(Auto, Dymo), Vega(HC), Megaron(AM), HE(Itek), Corvus, Claro	

	1	2	3	4	5	6	7	8	9	0
serif	X	86	X	X	X	X	•	X	X	X
proportion	169	179	187	196	•	X				
contrast	X	X	X	X	X	•				
arm style	•	X	X	X	X	X	209	X	X	
form	•	X	205	207	X	X				
midline	•	X	X	X	X	X	X	X		
x height	X	X	•	X						

ABCDEFGHIJ
KLMNOP
QRSTUVWXY
Z
abcdefghijkl
mnopqr
stuvwxyz
1234567890.
,;:''&!?$

Trade Gothic Condensed 48 point

ABCDEFGHIJKLMNOPQRST
UVWXYZ
abcdefghijklmnopqrstuvw
xyz
1234567890.,;:''&!?$

Trade Gothic Condensed Italic 24 point

PANOSE abegmoqst

(t1923) Trade Gothic Extracondensed 24 point

PANOSE abegmoqst

(t1919) Trade Gothic Bold Condensed 24 point

PANOSE abegmoqst

(t1921) Trade Gothic Bold Condensed Italic 24 point

PANOSE abegmoqst

(t1925) Trade Gothic Bold Extracondensed 24 point

Supplier	**Compugraphic 8400 Digital Typesetter**
Usage	**Display**
Similar Fonts	
Available Media	
Hot, Photo, Digital	
Alternate Names	
Trade Condensed(CG)	

	1	2	3	4	5	6	7	8	9	0
serif	X	86	X	X	X	X	●	X	X	X
proportion	(169)	(179)	(187)	(196)	●	X				
contrast	X	X	X	X	X	●				
arm style	●	X	X	X	X	X	209	X	X	
form	●	X	(205)	(207)	X	X				
midline	●	X	X	X	X	X	X	X		
x height	X	X	●	X						

ABCDEFGHIJKL MNOPQRSTUV WXYZ
abcdefghijklmno pqrstuvwxyz
1234567890.,;: ''&!?$

Akzidenz Grotesk Condensed 48 point

ABCDEFGHIJKLMNOPQRST
UVWXYZ
abcdefghijklmnopqrs
tuvwxyz
1234567890.,;:''&!?$

Akzidenz Grotesk Bold Condensed 24 point

ABCDEFGHIJKLMNOPQR
STUVWXYZ
abcdefghijklmnopqrstu
vwxyz
1234567890.,;:''&!?$

Akzidenz Grotesk Black Condensed 24 point

Supplier	Linotype 202 Digital Typesetter
Usage	Display
Similar Fonts	Anzeigen, Boreasterner
Available Media	
Hot, Photo, Digital	
Alternate Names	
Ad Grotesk, Grigat	

	1	2	3	4	5	6	7	8	9	0
serif	X	86	X	X	X	X	●	X	X	X
proportion	169	179	187	195	●	X				
contrast	X	X	X	X	X	●				
arm style	●	X	X	X	X	X	209	X	X	
form	X	X	●	X	X	X				
midline	●	X	X	X	X	X	X	X		
x height	X	●	205	X						

ABCDEFGHIJ
KLMNOP
QRSTUVWXY
Z
abcdefghijkl
mnopqr
stuvwxyz
1234567890
.,;:''&!?$

Univers Condensed 57 48 point

ABCDEFGHIJKLMNOPQRS
TUVWXYZ
abcdefghijklmnopqrstuvwx
yz
1234567890.,;:''&!?$

Univers Condensed Italic 58 24 point

PANOSE abegmoqst

Univers Light Condensed 47 24 point

PANOSE abegmoqst

Univers Light Condensed Italic 48 24 point

PANOSE abegmoqst

Univers Light Ultra Condensed 49 24 point

PANOSE abegmoqst

Univers Bold Condensed 67 24 point

PANOSE abegmoqst

Univers Bold Condensed Italic 68 24 point

Supplier	Compugraphic 8400 Digital Typesetter
Usage	Display
Similar Fonts	Block Condensed
Available Media	
Digital, Photo, Hot, DT, Bit	
Alternate Names	
Swiss 742(BS), Galaxy, UN(Itek)	

	1	2	3	4	5	6	7	8	9	0
serif	X	86	X	X	X	X	●	X	X	X
proportion	169	179	187	195	●	X				
contrast	X	X	X	X	X	●				
arm style	●	X	X	X	X	X	209	X	X	
form	X	X	●	X	X	X				
midline	●	X	X	X	X	X	X	X		
x height	X	●	205	X						

ABCDEFGHIJKL
MNOP
QRSTUVWXYZ
abcdefghijklmn
opqr
stuvwxyz
1234567890.,
;:''&!?$

Alpin Gothic 2 48 point

ABCDEFGHIJKLMNOPQRSTUVW
XYZ
abcdefghijklmnopqrstuvwxyz
1234567890.,;:''&!?$

Alpin Gothic 2 Italic 24 point

ABCDEFGHIJKLMNOPQRSTUVWXYZ
abcdefghijklmnopqrstuvwxyz
1234567890.,;:''&!?$

Alpin Gothic 1 24 point

PANOSE abegmoqst

Alpin Gothic 3 24 point

Supplier	Compugraphic 8400 Digital Typesetter
Usage	Display
Similar Fonts	
Available Media	
Digital, Hot, DT, Photo, Bit	
Alternate Names	
Alternate Gothic(Merg), Gothic 729(BS)	

	1	2	3	4	5	6	7	8	9	0
serif	X	86	X	X	X	X	●	X	X	X
proportion	169	179	187	195	●	X				
contrast	X	X	X	X	X	●				
arm style	●	X	X	X	X	X	209	X	X	
form	(199)	X	●	(207)	X	X				
midline	●	X	X	X	X	X	X	X		
x height	X	(203)	●	X						

ABCDEFGHI
JKLMNOPQ
RSTUVW
XYZ
abcdefghij
klmnopqrs
tuvwxyz
12345678
90.,;:"&!?$

Helvetica Compressed 42 point

ABCDEFGHIJKLMNOPQ
RSTUVWXYZ
abcdefghijklmnopqrst
uvwxyz
1234567890.,;:''&!?$

Helvetica Inserat 24 point

ABCDEFGHIJKLMNOPQ
RSTUVWXYZ
abcdefghijklmnopqrst
uvwxyz
1234567890.,;:''&!?$

Helvetica Inserat Italic 24 point

PANOSE abegmoqst
Helvetica Extra Compressed 24 point

PANOSE abegmoqst
Helvetica Ultra Compressed 24 point

Supplier	Linotronic 202 Digital Typesetter
Usage	Display
Similar Fonts	
Available Media	
Photo, Digital, Bit, DT	
Alternate Names	

Swiss 911(BS), Helios(CG), Triumvirate(CG), Geneva(Wang), Newton(Auto, Dymo), Vega(HC), Megaron(AM), HE(Itek), Corvus, Claro

	1	2	3	4	5	6	7	8	9	0
serif	X	86	X	X	X	X	●	X	X	X
proportion	169	179	187	195	●	X				
contrast	X	X	X	X	X	●				
arm style	●	X	X	X	X	X	209	X	X	
form	199	X	●	207	X	X				
midline	●	X	X	X	X	X	X	X		
x height	X	203	●	X						

ABCDEFGHIJKLMN
OPQRSTUVWXYZ
abcdefghijklmnopq
rstuvwxyz 12345
67890.,;"&!?$

Compacta 48 point

ABCDEFGHIJKLM
NOPQRSTUVWXYZ
abcdefghijklmnopqr
stuvwxyz 123456
7890.,;"&!?$

Compacta Black 24 point

PANOSE abegmoqst

Compacta Light 24 point

PANOSE abegmoqst

Compacta Italic 24 point

PANOSE abegmoqst

Compacta Bold 24 point

PANOSE abegmoqst

Compacta Bold Italic 24 point

Supplier	Alphatype CRS Digital Typesetter
Usage	Display
Similar Fonts	Aurora Grotesque
Available Media	
Photo, Digital, DT	
Alternate Names	

	1	2	3	4	5	6	7	8	9	0
serif	X	86	X	X	X	X	•	X	X	X
proportion	169	179	191	195	•	X				
contrast	X	X	X	X	X	•				
arm style	•	X	X	X	X	X	209	X	X	
form	199	X	205	•	X	X				
midline	•	X	X	X	X	X	X	X		
x height	X	X	•	X						

ABCDEFGHIJKL MNOPQRSTUV WXYZ abcdefghijklm nopqrstuvw xyz 1234567890 .,;:"&!?$

ITC Machine 48 point

ABCDEFGHIJKLMNO PQRSTUVWXYZ abcdefghijklmnop qrstuvwxyz 1234567890 .,;:"&!?$

ITC Machine Bold 36 point

Supplier	**Compugraphic 8400 Digital Typesetter**
Usage	**Display**
Similar Fonts	**Rapporter**
Available Media	
Photo, Digital, PS, Bit, DT	
Alternate Names	
Square 880(BS)	

	1	2	3	4	5	6	7	8	9	0
serif	X	86	X	X	X	X	●	X	X	X
proportion	169	179	187	195	●	X				
contrast	X	X	X	X	X	●				
arm style	●	X	X	X	X	X	209	X	X	
form	X	X	X	X	X	●				
midline	●	X	X	X	X	X	X	X		
x height	X	X	X	●						

ABCDEFGHIJK LMNOP QRSTUVWXYZ abcdefghijklm nopqr stuvwxyz 1234567890 .,;:''&!?$

Futura Medium Condensed 48 point

ABCDEFGHIJKLMNOPQRSTUVW XYZ
abcdefghijklmnopqrstuvwxyz
1234567890.,;:''&!?$

Futura Light Condensed 24 point

ABCDEFGHIJKLMNOPQR STUVWXYZ abcdefghijklmnopqrstuv wxyz 1234567890.,;:''&!?$

Futura Bold Condensed 24 point

PANOSE abegmoqst

Futura Extra Black Condensed 24 point

Supplier	**Compugraphic 8400 Digital Typesetter**
Usage	**Display**
Similar Fonts	
Available Media	
Hot, Photo, Digital, Bit	
Alternate Names	
Futura Condensed II(CG), Geometric 211(BS), FU(Itek), Future, Photura(Auto, Dymo), Sirius, Spartan(Merg), Techno(AM, Auto, Dymo), Tempo, Twentieth-Century	

	1	2	3	4	5	6	7	8	9	0
serif	X	87	X	X	158	X	•	X	X	X
proportion	171	184	194	X	•	X				
contrast	X	X	X	X	X	•				
arm style	199	X	X	X	X	X	•	X	X	
form	•	X	X	X	X	X				
midline	•	X	X	211	X	X	X	X		
x height	X	•	X	X						

ABCDEFGH IJKLMNO PQRST UVWXYZ abcdefghijk lmnopqrs tuvwxyz 1234567890 ,.;:"&!?$

Gill Sans Condensed 48 point

ABCDEFGHIJKLMNOPQ RSTUVWXYZ abcdefghijklmnopqrst uvwxyz 1234567890.,;:"&!?$

Gill Sans Bold Condensed 24 point

ABCDEFGHIJKLMNOP QRSTUVWXYZ abcdefghijklmnopqrstu vwxyz 1234567890.,;:" &!?$

Gill Sans Extra Bold Condensed 24 point

PANOSE abegmoqst

Gill Sans Ultra Bold Condensed 24 point

Supplier	Linotype 202 Digital Typesetter
Usage	Display
Similar Fonts	Bell Centenial, Spartan Condensed
Available Media	
Photo, Digital, DT, Bit	
Alternate Names	
Humanist 521(BS), Eric, Glib(Alpha), Graphic Gothic(Wang)	

	1	2	3	4	5	6	7	8	9	0
serif	X	(87)	X	X	158	X	•	X	X	X
proportion	(171)	184	194	X	•	X				
contrast	X	X	X	X	X	•				
arm style	199	X	X	X	X	X	•	X	X	
form	•	X	X	X	X	X				
midline	•	X	X	(211)	X	X	X	X		
x height	X	•	X	X						

ABCDEFG
HIJKLMNO
PQRSTUVW
XYZ
abcdefghijkl
mnopqrstu
vwxyz
1234567890
.,;:"&!?$

Spartan Medium Condensed 48 point

ABCDEFGHIJKLMNOPQRS
TUVWXYZ
abcdefghijklmnopqr
stuvwxyz
1234567890.,;:"&!?$

Spartan Bold Condensed 24 point

PANOSE abegmoqst

Spartan Book Condensed 24 point

PANOSE abegmoqst

Spartan Heavy Condensed 24 point

PANOSE abegmoqst

Spartan Black Condensed 24 point

PANOSE abegmoqst

Spartan Extra Black Condensed 24 point

Supplier	Linotronic 202 Digital Typesetter
Usage	**Display**
Similar Fonts	**Block Condensed**
Available Media	
Digital, Photo, Bit	
Alternate Names	
Geometric 212(BS), Futura(Alpha, BH, CG, HC, Merg), Techno(AM, Auto Dymo), Photura(Auto, Dymo), Future, FU(Itek), Sirius, Tempo, Twenty-Cent., Utica(Wang)	

	1	2	3	4	5	6	7	8	9	0
serif	X	87	X	X	158	X	•	X	X	X
proportion	(174)	184	194	X	•	X				
contrast	X	X	X	X	X	•				
arm style	199	X	X	X	X	X	•	X	X	
form	•	X	X	X	X	X				
midline	(209)	X	X	•	X	X	X	X		
x height	X	•	X	X						

ABCDEFGHI JKLMNOP QRSTUVW XYZ abcdefghijkl mnopqr stuvwxyz 123456789 0.,;:''&!?$

Symphony 42 point

ABCDEFGHIJKLMNO
PQRSTUVWXYZ
abcdefghijklmnopqrst
uvwxyz
1234567890.,;:''&!?$

Symphony Italic 24 point

ABCDEFGHIJKLMNO
PQRSTUVWXYZ
abcdefghijklmnopqrst
uvwxyz
1234567890.,;:''&!?$

Symphony Bold 24 point

PANOSE abegmoqst

Symphony Black 24 point

PANOSE abegmoqst

Symphony Ultra 24 point

Supplier	Compugraphic 8400 Digital Typesetter
Usage	Display, Text
Similar Fonts	
Available Media	
Photo, Digital	
Alternate Names	

	1	2	3	4	5	6	7	8	9	0
serif	37	X	X	X	X	X	170	●	X	236
proportion	●	X	X	X	X	215				
contrast	X	X	X	X	X	●				
arm style	X	X	X	●	X	X	214	X	X	
form	●	X	X	X	X	X				
midline	●	X	X	X	X	X	X	X		
x height	X	●	X	X						

ABCDEFG
HIJKLMN
OPQRSTU
VWXYZ
abcdefghij
klmnopqrs
tuvwxyz
12345678
90.,;:''&!?$

Syntax 46 point

ABCDEFGHIJKLMNO
PQRSTUVWXYZ
abcdefghijklmnopqrst
uvwxyz
1234567890.,;:''&!?$

Syntax Italic 24 point

ABCDEFGHIJKLMNO
PQRSTUVWXYZ
abcdefghijklmnopqrs
tuvwxyz
1234567890.,;:''&!?$

Syntax Bold 24 point

PANOSE abegmoqst

Syntax Black

PANOSE abegmoqst

Syntax Ultra Black 24 point

Supplier	Linotronic 202 Digital Typesetter
Usage	Text, Display
Similar Fonts	Granby
Available Media	
Photo, Digital	
Alternate Names	

	1	2	3	4	5	6	7	8	9	0
serif	37	X	X	X	X	X	170	•	X	236
proportion	•	X	X	X	X	215				
contrast	X	X	X	X	X	•				
arm style	X	X	X	•	X	X	214	X	X	
form	•	X	X	X	X	X				
midline	•	X	X	X	X	X	X	X		
x height	X	•	X	X						

ABCDEFGHI JKLMNOP QRSTUVWX YZ abcdefghij klmnopqr stuvwxyz 123456789 0.,;:''&!?$

ITC Kabel Medium 42 point

ABCDEFGHIJKLMNO
PQRSTUVWXYZ
abcdefghijklmnopqr
stuvwxyz
1234567890.,;:''&!?$

ITC Kabel Demi 24 point

**ABCDEFGHIJKLMNO
PQRSTUVWXYZ
abcdefghijklmnopqr
stuvwxyz
1234567890.,;:''&!?$**

ITC Kabel Bold 23 point

PANOSE abegmoqst

ITC Kabel Book 24 point

PANOSE abegmoqst

ITC Kabel Ultra 24 point

Supplier	Compugraphic 8400 Digital Typesetter
Usage	Display, Text
Similar Fonts	Cable, Sally Mae
Available Media	
Digital, Photo, Hot, Bit	
Alternate Names	
Geometric 731(BS)	

	1	2	3	4	5	6	7	8	9	0
serif	X	69	96	X	X	X	171	●	(221)	237
proportion	●	X	X	X	X	X				
contrast	X	X	X	X	X	●				
arm style	X	X	X	212	X	X	●	X	X	
form	●	X	X	X	X	X				
midline	X	●	X	X	X	X	X	X		
x height	X	X	●	X						

ABCDEFGH
IJKLMNOP
QRSTUV
WXYZ

ABCDEFGHI

JKLMNOPQR

STUVWXYZ

1234567890

.,;:'"&!?$

Orator 48 point

ABCDEFGHI

JKLMNOPQR

STUVWXYZ

abcdefghi

jklmnopqr

stuvwxyz

1234567890

.,;:'"&!?$

Orator Oblique 36 point

Supplier	**Linotype 100 PostScript**
Usage	**Text**
Similar Fonts	
Available Media	
Photo, Digital, PS	
Alternate Names	

	1	2	3	4	5	6	7	8	9	0
serif	X	X	X	X	X	X	X	•	X	X
proportion	212	X	X	X	X	•				
contrast	X	X	X	X	X	•				
arm style	X	X	X	•	X	X	X	X	X	
form	•	X	X	X	X	X				
midline	•	X	X	X	X	X	X	X		
x height	X	X	•	X						

ABCDEFGH
IJKLMNOP
QRSTUVW
XYZ
abcdefghijkl
mnopqr
stuvwxyz
123456789
0.,;:''&!?$

Albertus Medium 42 point

ABCDEFGHIJKLMNOP
QRSTUVWXYZ
abcdefghijklmnopqrstuv
wxyz
1234567890.,;:''&!?$

Albertus Medium Oblique 23 point

PANOSE abegmoqst

Albertus Book 24 point

PANOSE abegmoqst

Albertus Book Oblique 24 point

PANOSE abegmoqst

Albertus Bold 24 point

PANOSE abegmoqst

Albertus Extra Bold 24 point

Supplier	Compugraphic 8400 Digital Typesetter
Usage	Display
Similar Fonts	Aurelio, Triplett
Available Media	
Hot, DT, Digital	
Alternate Names	

	1	2	3	4	5	6	7	8	9	0
serif	X	X	X	X	149	X	X	X	•	X
proportion	•	X	X	X	X	X				
contrast	•	X	X	X	X	X				
arm style	•	X	X	X	X	X	X	X	X	
form	•	X	X	X	X	X				
midline	X	•	218	X	X	X	X	X		
x height	X	X	•	X						

ABCDEFG HIJKLMN OPQRST UVWXYZ abcdefghij klmnopqr stuvwxyz 1234567 890.,;''&

Romic Medium 48 point

ABCDEFGHIJKLMNO
PQRSTUVWXYZ
abcdefghijklmnopqrs
tuvwxyz1234567
890.,;''&!?$

Romic Light 24 point

ABCDEFGHIJKLMNO
PQRSTUVWXYZ
abcdefghijklmnopqrs
tuvwxyz1234567
890.,;''&!?$

Romic Light Italic 24 point

PANOSE abegmoqst

Romic Bold 24 point

PANOSE abegmoq

Romic Extra Bold 24 point

Supplier	**Alphatype CRS Digital Typesetter**
Usage	**Display, Text**
Similar Fonts	
Available Media	
Photo, Digital, DT	
Alternate Names	

	1	2	3	4	5	6	7	8	9	0
serif	X	X	X	X	149	X	X	X	•	X
proportion	•	X	X	X	X	X				
contrast	•	X	X	X	X	X				
arm style	•	X	X	X	X	X	X	X	X	
form	•	X	X	X	X	X				
midline	X	•	(218)	X	X	X	X	X		
x height	X	X	•	X						

ABCDEFGHI JKLMNOP QRSTUVW XYZ abcdefghij klmnopqr stuvwxyz 12345678 90.,;:''&!?$

Friz Quadrata 42 point

ABCDEFGHIJKL MNOPQRSTUV WXYZ abcdefghijklm nopqrstuvwxyz 1234567890., ;:''&!?$

Friz Quadrata Bold 32 point

Supplier	Compugraphic 8400 Digital Typesetter	
Usage	Text, Display	
Similar Fonts	Argonaut	
Available Media		
Photo, Digital, Bit, DT		
Alternate Names		
Flareserif 861(BS)		

	1	2	3	4	5	6	7	8	9	0
serif	X	X	X	X	149	X	X	X	•	X
proportion	•	X	X	X	X	X				
contrast	•	X	X	X	X	X				
arm style	•	X	X	X	X	X	X	X	X	
form	•	X	X	X	X	X				
midline	X	216	•	X	X	X	X	X		
x height	X	X	•	X						

ABCDEFG HIJKLMN OPQRST UVWXYZ abcdefghi jklmnopq rstuvwxyz 123456789 0.,;:''&!?$

Optima Medium 46 point

PANOSE abegmoqst

Optima 24 point

PANOSE abegmoqst

Optima Italic 24 point

PANOSE abegmoqst

Optima Medium Italic 24 point

PANOSE abegmoqst

Optima Bold 24 point

PANOSE abegmoqst

Optima Bold Italic 24 point

PANOSE abegmoqst

Optima Black 24 point

PANOSE abegmoqst

Optima Black Italic 24 point

Supplier	**Linotronic 202 Digital Typesetter**
Usage	**Text, Display**
Similar Fonts	**Pascal**
Available Media	
Digital, Photo, DT, Hot, Bit, PS	
Alternate Names	
Zapf Humanist 601(BS), Omega(CG), Athena, Chelmsford(AM, Auto, Dymo), Optimist(Auto), Zenith(HC), OP(Itek), Musica(Alpha),Theme(IBM), Orleans(Wang)	

	1	2	3	4	5	6	7	8	9	0
serif	(23)	68	93	X	X	X	(168)	X	•	X
proportion	•	224	X	X	235	X				
contrast	X	•	X	X	X	X				
arm style	X	X	•	X	X	X	X	X	X	
form	•	X	X	X	X	X				
midline	X	•	X	X	X	X	X	X		
x height	X	•	X	X						

ABCDEFG HIJKLMN OPQRSTU VWXYZ abcdefghij klmnopqrs tuvwxyz 1234567 890.,;"&!?

ITC Symbol Medium 48 point

PANOSE abegmoqst

ITC Symbol Book 24 point

PANOSE abegmoqst

ITC Symbol Book Italic 24 point

PANOSE abegmoqst

ITC Symbol Medium Italic 24 point

PANOSE abegmoqst

ITC Symbol Bold 24 point

PANOSE abegmoqst

ITC Symbol Bold Italic 24 point

PANOSE abegmoq

ITC Symbol Black 24 point

PANOSE abegmoq

ITC Symbol Black Italic 24 point

Supplier	**Alphatype CRS Digital Typesetter**
Usage	**Text, Display**
Similar Fonts	
Available Media	
Photo, Digital, Bit	
Alternate Names	
Copperplate 721(BS)	

	1	2	3	4	5	6	7	8	9	0
serif	X	(70)	96	X	X	X	171	214	•	237
proportion	•	(226)	X	(234)	X	X				
contrast	X	X	X	X	X	•				
arm style	X	X	X	X	X	X	•	223	X	
form	•	X	X	X	X	X				
midline	•	(221)	X	X	X	X	X	X		
x height	X	X	•	X						

ABCDEFG HIJKLMN OPQRST UVWXYZ abcdefghi jklmnopq rstuvwxy 1234567 890.,;'&!?

ITC Elan 48 point

PANOSE abegmoqst

ITC Elan Book 24 point

PANOSE abegmoqst

ITC Elan Book Italic 24 point

PANOSE abegmoqst

ITC Elan Medium Italic 24 point

PANOSE abegmoqst

ITC Elan Bold 24 point

PANOSE abegmoq

ITC Elan Bold Italic 24 point

PANOSE abegmoq

ITC Elan Black 24 point

PANOSE abegmo

ITC Elan Black Italic 24 point

Supplier	**Alphatype CRS Digital Typesetter**
Usage	**Text, Display**
Similar Fonts	**Cursillo**
Available Media	
Photo, Digital	
Alternate Names	

	1	2	3	4	5	6	7	8	9	0
serif	X	69	96	X	X	X	171	(214)	•	237
proportion	•	226	X	234	X	X				
contrast	X	X	X	X	X	•				
arm style	X	X	X	X	X	X	•	223	X	
form	•	X	X	X	X	X				
midline	(220)	•	X	X	X	X	X	X		
x height	X	X	•	X						

ITC Serif Gothic

ABCDEFG
HIJKLMNO
PQRSTUV
WXYZ abc
defghijkl
mnopqrst
uvwxyz
1234567
890.,;"&!?$

ITC Serif Gothic 48 point

ABCDEFGHIJKLMNO
PQRSTUVWXYZ
abcdefghijklmnopq
rstuvwxyz
1234567890.,;"&!?$

ITC Serif Gothic Heavy 24 point

PANOSE abegmoqst

ITC Serif Gothic Light 24 point

PANOSE abegmoqst

ITC Serif Gothic Bold 24 point

PANOSE abegmoqst

ITC Serif Gothic Extra Bold 24 point

PANOSE abegmoqst

ITC Serif Gothic Black 24 point

Supplier	Alphatype CRS Digital Typesetter
Usage	Display
Similar Fonts	Sleek Gothic
Available Media	
Digital, DT, Photo, Bit	
Alternate Names	
Line Gothic(Wang), Copperplate 701(BS)	

	1	2	3	4	5	6	7	8	9	0
serif	X	69	96	X	X	X	171	**214**	•	237
proportion	•	226	X	234	X	X				
contrast	X	X	X	X	X	•				
arm style	X	X	X	X	X	X	•	223	X	
form	•	X	X	X	X	X				
midline	**220**	•	X	X	X	X	X	X		
x height	X	X	•	X						

ABCDEFGHI JKLMNOPQ RSTUVWX YZ abcd efghijklmno pqrstuvwx yz 1234567 890.,;"&!?$

ITC Goudy Sans Medium 48 point

PANOSE abegmoqst

ITC Goudy Sans Book 24 point

PANOSE abegmoqst

ITC Goudy Sans Book Italic 24 point

PANOSE abegmoqst

ITC Goudy Sans Medium Italic 24 point

PANOSE abegmoqst

ITC Goudy Sans Bold 24 point

PANOSE abegmoqst

ITC Goudy Sans Bold Italic 24 point

PANOSE abegmoqst

ITC Goudy Sans Black 24 point

PANOSE abegmoqst

ITC Goudy Sans Black Italic 24 point

Supplier	**Alphatype CRS Digital Typesetter**
Usage	**Display**
Similar Fonts	**Hugo Sans**
Available Media	
Photo, Digital	
Alternate Names	

	1	2	3	4	5	6	7	8	9	0
serif	X	X	X	X	X	X	X	X	•	X
proportion	•	X	X	X	X	X				
contrast	X	X	X	X	X	•				
arm style	X	X	X	X	X	X	220	•	X	
form	X	•	X	X	X	X				
midline	•	X	X	X	X	X	X	X		
x height	X	•	X	X						

ABCDEFG HIJKLMNO PQRSTUV WXYZ abc defghijkl mnopqrstu vwxyz 1234567 890.,;"&!?

Souvenir Gothic Medium 48 point

ABCDEFGHIJKLMNO
PQRSTUVWXYZ
abcdefghijklmnopqrst
uvwxyz
1234567890.,;:''&!?$

Souvenir Gothic Medium Italic 23 point

PANOSE abegmoqst

Souvenir Gothic Light 24 point

PANOSE abegmoqst

Souvenir Gothic Light Italic 24 point

PANOSE abegmoqst

Souvenir Gothic Demi 24 point

PANOSE abegmoqst

Souvenir Gothic Demi Italic 24 point

Supplier	Alphatype CRS Digital Typesetter
Usage	Text, Display
Similar Fonts	
Available Media	
Photo, Digital, DT	
Alternate Names	

	1	2	3	4	5	6	7	8	9	0
serif	39	72	99	134	X	162	X	X	•	X
proportion	219	•	X	X	235	X				
contrast	X	•	X	X	X	X				
arm style	X	X	•	X	X	X	X	X	X	
form	•	X	X	X	X	X				
midline	X	X	•	X	X	X	X	X		
x height	X	•	X	X						

ABCDEFG HIJKLMN OPQRSTU VWXYZ

abcdefghijk lmnopqrst uvwxyz 123456789 0.,;:""&!?$

Poppl-Laudatio Medium 48 point

PANOSE abegmoqst
Poppl-Laudatio Light 24 point

PANOSE abegmoqst
Poppl-Laudatio Light Italic 24 point

PANOSE abegmoqst
Poppl-Laudatio 24 point

PANOSE abegmoqst
Poppl-Laudatio Italic 24 point

PANOSE abegmoqst
Poppl-Laudatio Medium Italic 24 point

PANOSE abegmoqst
Poppl-Laudatio Bold 24 point

PANOSE abegmoqst
Poppl-Laudatio Bold Italic 24 point

Supplier	**Alphatype CRS Digital Typesetter**
Usage	**Text, Display**
Similar Fonts	**Baker Signet, Callorte**
Available Media	
Photo, Digital	
Alternate Names	

	1	2	3	4	5	6	7	8	9	0
serif	39	73	99	134	X	162	X	X	●	X
proportion	219	●	X	X	(235)	X				
contrast	X	●	X	X	X	X				
arm style	X	X	●	X	X	X	X	X	X	
form	X	●	X	X	X	X				
midline	●	X	X	X	X	X	X	X		
x height	X	X	●	X						

ABCDEFG HIJKLMN OPQRSTU VWXYZ

abcdefghijk lmnopqrst uvwxyz 123456789 0.,;:"&!?$

Flange Medium 48 point

PANOSE abegmoqst
Flange Light 24 point

PANOSE abegmoqst
Flange Light Italic 24 point

PANOSE abegmoqst
Flange 24 point

PANOSE abegmoqst
Flange Italic 24 point

PANOSE abegmoqst
Flange Medium Italic 24 point

PANOSE abegmoqst
Flange Bold 24 point

PANOSE abegmoqst
Flange Bold Italic 24 point

Supplier	Alphatype CRS Digital Typesetter
Usage	Display, Text
Similar Fonts	
Available Media	
Photo, Digital	
Alternate Names	

	1	2	3	4	5	6	7	8	9	0
serif	X	77	X	X	X	X	184	X	•	X
proportion	220	•	X	234	X	X				
contrast	X	X	X	X	X	•				
arm style	X	X	X	X	X	X	•	X	229	
form	•	228	X	X	X	X				
midline	•	X	X	X	X	X	X	X		
x height	X	X	•	X						

ABCDEFG
HIJKLMNO
PQRSTUV
WXYZ
abcdefghijk
lmnopqrstu
vwxyz
123456789
0.,;:''&!?$

Icone 55 42 point

PANOSE abegmoqst

Icone Light 45 24 point

PANOSE abegmoqst

Icone Light Italic 46 24 point

PANOSE abegmoqst

Icone Italic 56 24 point

PANOSE abegmoqst

Icone Bold 65 24 point

PANOSE abegmoqst

Icone Bold Italic 66 24 point

PANOSE abegmoqst

Icone Extra Black 86 24 point

PANOSE abegmoqst

Icone Extra Black 85 24 point

Supplier	**Linotronic 202 Digital Typesetter**
Usage	**Text, Display**
Similar Fonts	**Friz Quadrata**
Available Media	
Photo, Digital	
Alternate Names	

	1	2	3	4	5	6	7	8	9	0
serif	X	(77)	X	X	X	X	184	X	•	X
proportion	(220)	•	X	(234)	X	X				
contrast	X	X	X	X	X	•				
arm style	X	X	X	X	X	X	•	X	229	
form	•	(228)	X	X	X	X				
midline	•	X	X	X	X	X	X	X		
x height	X	X	•	X						

ABCDEFG
HIJKLMN
OPQRSTU
VWXYZ
abcdefghij
klmnopqrs
tuvwxyz
1234567
890.,;"&!?$

ITC Quorum Medium 48 point

ABCDEFGHIJKLMNO
PQRSTUVWXYZ
abcdefghijklmnopq
rstuvwxyz
1234567890.,;"&!?$

ITC Quorum Book 24 point

ABCDEFGHIJKLMNO
PQRSTUVWXYZ
abcdefghijklmnopq
rstuvwxyz
1234567890.,;"&!?$

ITC Quorum Bold 24 point

PANOSE abegmoqst

ITC Quorum Light 24 point

PANOSE abegmoqst

ITC Quorum Black 24 point

Supplier	Alphatype CRS Digital Typesetter
Usage	Display
Similar Fonts	Tamil
Available Media	
Digital, Photo, DT, Bit	
Alternate Names	
Flareserif 851(BS)	

	1	2	3	4	5	6	7	8	9	0
serif	X	77	X	X	X	X	184	X	•	X
proportion	220	•	X	234	X	X				
contrast	X	X	X	X	X	•				
arm style	X	X	X	X	X	X	•	X	229	
form	226	•	X	X	X	X				
midline	•	X	X	X	X	X	X	X		
x height	X	X	•	X						

ABCDEFGHI
JKLMNOP
QRSTUVWX
YZ
abcdefghijkl
mnopqr
stuvwxyz
123456789
0.,;:''&!?$

Shannon Book 42 point

ABCDEFGHIJKLMN
OPQRSTUVWXYZ
abcdefghijklmnopqrstuv
wxyz
1234567890.,;:''&!?$

Shannon Book Oblique 24 point

ABCDEFGHIJKLMNOPQ
RSTUVWXYZ
abcdefghijklmnopqrst
uvwxyz
1234567890.,;:''&!?$

Shannon Bold 21 point

Supplier	Compugraphic 8400 Digital Typesetter
Usage	Text, Display
Similar Fonts	Continental
Available Media	
Photo, Digital	
Alternate Names	

	1	2	3	4	5	6	7	8	9	0
serif	X	X	X	X	X	X	X	X	●	X
proportion	X	●	X	X	X	X				
contrast	X	X	X	X	X	●				
arm style	X	X	X	X	X	X	226	X	●	
form	X	X	X	X	●	X				
midline	X	X	●	X	X	X	X	X		
x height	X	●	X	X						

ABCDEFG HIJKLMNO PQRSTUV WXYZ abc defghijklm nopqrstuv wxyz 123 4567890 .,;"&!?

Bluejack Medium 42 point

ABCDEFGHIJKLMNOP QRSTUVWXYZ abcdefghijklmnopq rstuvwxyz 1234567890.,;"&!?$

Bluejack Light 24 point

ABCDEFGHIJKLMNO PQRSTUVWXYZ abc defghijklmnopqrstu vwxyz 1234567 890.,;"&!?$

Bluejack Bold 24 point

PANOSE abegmoqst

Bluejack Light Italic 24 point

Supplier	**Alphatype CRS Digital Typesetter**
Usage	**Display, Text**
Similar Fonts	
Available Media	
Digital	
Alternate Names	

	1	2	3	4	5	6	7	8	9	0
serif	X	X	(113)	X	X	(165)	X	X	•	X
proportion	X	X	•	X	X	X				
contrast	•	X	X	X	X	X				
arm style	X	X	•	X	X	X	X	X	X	
form	•	X	X	X	X	X				
midline	•	X	X	X	X	X	X	X		
x height	X	X	•	X						

ABCDEF
GHIJKLM
NOPQRST
UVWXYZ
abcdefghij
klmnopqr
stuvwxyz
123456789
0.,;:"&!?$

Modula Medium 42 point

ABCDEFGHIJKLM
NOPQRSTUVWXYZ
abcdefghijklm
nopqrstuvwxyz
1234567890.,;:"&!?$

Modula 24 point

ABCDEFGHIJKLM
NOPQRSTUVWXYZ
abcdefghijklm
nopqrstuvwxyz
1234567890.,;:"&!?$

Modula Bold 24 point

PANOSE abegmoqst

Modula Extra Bold 24 point

Supplier	**Linotronic 202 Digital Typesetter**
Usage	**Display**
Similar Fonts	
Available Media	
Photo, Digital	
Alternate Names	
Serpentine(Alpha)	

	1	2	3	4	5	6	7	8	9	0
serif	X	80	123	X	X	X	X	X	•	X
proportion	X	X	•	X	X	X				
contrast	X	•	X	X	X	X				
arm style	X	X	X	X	•	X	X	X	X	
form	X	X	X	•	X	X				
midline	•	X	X	X	X	X	X	X		
x height	X	X	•	X						

ABCDEFG HIJKLMN OPQRSTU VWXYZ

abcdefghijk lmnopqrst uvwxyz 123456789 0.,;:"&!?$

American Gothic Medium 36 point

ABCDEFGHIJKLM NOPQRSTUVWXY abcdefghijklmnop qrstuvwxyz 1234567890.,;"&!?

American Gothic Medium Italic 24 point

PANOSE abegmo

American Gothic Light 24 point

PANOSE abegmoq

American Gothic Light Italic 24 point

PANOSE abegmo

American Gothic Bold 24 point

Supplier	**Alphatype CRS Digital Typesetter**
Usage	**Display, Text**
Similar Fonts	**Ashley Crawford**
Available Media	
Digital	
Alternate Names	
American Classic (CG); Americana (Merg)	

	1	2	3	4	5	6	7	8	9	0
serif	X	82	X	X	X	X	192	X	•	**240**
proportion	X	X	•	X	X	X				
contrast	X	X	X	X	X	•				
arm style	X	X	X	•	X	X	X	X	X	
form	•	X	X	X	X	X				
midline	•	X	X	X	X	X	X	X		
x height	X	X	•	**233**						

ABCDEFG
HIJKLMNO
P
QRSTUVW
XYZ
12345678
90.,;:''&!?$

Copperplate Gothic Light 36 point

ABCDEFGHIJKLMNO
PQRSTUVWXYZ
1234567890.,;:''&!?$

Copperplate Gothic Heavy 19 point

ABCDEFGHIJKLMNO
PQRSTUVWXYZ

ABCDEFGHIJKLMNOPQR
STUVWXYZ

1234567890.,;:'' (–($

Copperplate Gothic No.4, No.3 24 point

PANOSE ABEGMOQST

Copperplate Gothic Bold No.4, No.3 24 point

Supplier	**Compugraphic 8400 Digital Typesetter**
Usage	**Display**
Similar Fonts	**Steelplate, Egypteinne Copperplate**
Available Media	
Digital, DT, Photo, Hot, Bit	
Alternate Names	
Copper Light, Copperplate(Alpha, BH, CG, Merg), Forma Gothic(Dymo), Gothic No. 31(HC), Lining Plate Gothic(Ludlow), Copperplate 001(BS)	

	1	2	3	4	5	6	7	8	9	0
serif	X	82	X	X	X	X	192	X	●	240
proportion	X	X	●	X	X	X				
contrast	X	X	X	X	X	●				
arm style	X	X	X	●	X	X	X	X	X	
form	●	X	X	X	X	X				
midline	●	X	X	X	X	X	X	X		
x height	X	X	(232)	●						

ABCDE
FGHIJK
LMNOP
QRSTU
VWXYZ
abcdefg
hijklmn
opqrstuv
wxyz
123456

ITC Newtext Regular 48 point

PANOSE abegmoq
ITC Newtext Light 24 point

PANOSE abegmoq
ITC Newtext Light Italic 24 point

PANOSE abegmo
ITC Newtext Book 24 point

PANOSE abegmoq
ITC Newtext Regular Italic 24 point

PANOSE abegm
ITC Newtext Demi 24 point

PANOSE abegm
ITC Newtext Demi Italic 24 point

Supplier	**Linotronic 300 Laser Typesetter**
Usage	**Text, Display**
Similar Fonts	
Available Media	
Digital, Photo, Bit	
Alternate Names	
Copperplate 421(BS)	

	1	2	3	4	5	6	7	8	9	0
serif	X	X	X	X	X	X	X	X	•	X
proportion	220	226	X	•	X	X				
contrast	X	X	X	X	X	•				
arm style	X	X	X	X	X	X	•	X	X	
form	•	X	X	X	X	X				
midline	•	X	X	X	X	X	X	X		
x height	X	X	•	X						

ABCDEFG
HIJKLMN
OPQRSTU
VWXYZ

abcdefghijk
lmnopqrst
uvwxyz
123456789
0.,;:"&!?$

Poppl-Laudatio Medium Condensed 48 point

ABCDEFGHIJKLMNO
PQRSTUVWXYZ
abcdefghijklmnopqrstu
vwxyz
1234567890.,;:"&!?$

Poppl-Laudatio Light Condensed 24 point

ABCDEFGHIJKLMNO
PQRSTUVWXYZ
abcdefghijklmnopqrstu
vwxyz
1234567890.,;:"&!?$

Poppl-Laudatio Condensed 24 point

PANOSE abegmoqst

Poppl-Laudatio Bold Condensed 24 point

Supplier	Alphatype CRS Digital Typesetter
Usage	Display, Text
Similar Fonts	
Available Media	
Photo, Digital	
Alternate Names	

	1	2	3	4	5	6	7	8	9	0
serif	X	X	126	X	157	X	198	X	•	X
proportion	219	225	X	X	•	X				
contrast	X	•	X	X	X	X				
arm style	X	X	•	X	X	X	X	X	X	
form	X	•	X	X	X	X				
midline	•	X	X	X	X	X	X	X		
x height	X	X	•	X						

ABCDEFG
HIJKLMNO
PQRSTUV
WXYZ
abcdefghij
klmnopqrs
tuvwxyz
12345678
90.,;:"&!?$

Wexford Medium 48 point

ABCDEFGHIJKLMNOP
QRSTUVWXYZ
abcdefghijklmnopqrstu
vuwxyz
1234567890.,;:"&!?$

Wexford 24 point

ABCDEFGHIJKLMNOP
QRSTUVWXYZ
abcdefghijklmnopqrst
uvwxyz
1234567890.,;:"&!?$

Wexford Bold 24 point

PANOSE abegmoqst

Wexford Ultra Bold 24 point

Supplier	Linotronic 202 Digital Typesetter
Usage	Display
Similar Fonts	Germanic Sans
Available Media	
Photo, Digital	
Alternate Names	

	1	2	3	4	5	6	7	8	9	0
serif	37	X	X	X	X	X	170	212	X	●
proportion	●	X	240	X	X	X				
contrast	X	X	X	X	X	●				
arm style	X	X	X	●	X	X	237	X	X	
form	●	X	X	X	X	X				
midline	X	X	X	X	X	X	X	●		
x height	X	X	●	X						

ABCDEFG HIJKLMN OPQRSTUV WXYZ abcdefghijk lmnopqrstuv wxyz 123456789 0.,;:''&!?$

Harry Plain 48 point

ABCDEFGHIJKLMNOPQ RSTUVWXYZ abcdefghijklmnopqrstuv wxyz 1234567890.,;:''&!?$

Harry Heavy 24 point

ABCDEFGHIJKLMNOP QRSTUVWXYZ abcdefghijklmnopqrstu vwxyz 1234567890.,;:''&!?$

Harry Fat 24 point

PANOSE abegmoqst

Harry Thin 24 point

PANOSE abegmoqst

Harry Obese 24 point

Supplier	**Linotronic 202 Digital Typesetter**
Usage	**Display**
Similar Fonts	**Poppo Black, Tabasco**
Available Media	
Photo, Digital, DT	
Alternate Names	

	1	2	3	4	5	6	7	8	9	0
serif	X	69	96	X	X	X	171	214	221	●
proportion	●	X	X	X	X	X				
contrast	X	X	X	X	X	●				
arm style	X	X	X	236	X	X	●	X	X	
form	●	X	X	X	X	X				
midline	X	●	X	X	X	X	X	X		
x height	X	●	X	X						

ABCDEFGH
IJKLMNOP
QRSTUVW
XYZ abcde
fghijklmno
pqrstuvwx
yz 123456
7890.,;"&!?

ITC Bauhaus Medium 48 point

ABCDEFGHIJKLMNOP
QRSTUVWXYZ abcdef
ghijklmnopqrstuvwxyz
1234567890.,;"&!?$

ITC Bauhaus Light 24 point

ABCDEFGHIJKLMNO
PQRSTUVWXYZ
abcdefghijklmnopq
rstuvwxyz
1234567890.,;"&!?$

ITC Bauhaus Demi 24 point

PANOSE abegmoqst

ITC Bauhaus Bold 24 point

PANOSE abegmoqst

ITC Bauhaus Heavy 24 point

Supplier	Alphatype CRS Digital Typesetter
Usage	Display
Similar Fonts	Organ Grinder
Available Media	
Digital, DT, Photo, Bit	
Alternate Names	
Geometric 752(BS)	

	1	2	3	4	5	6	7	8	9	0
serif	X	69	96	X	X	X	171	214	220	•
proportion	•	X	X	X	X	X				
contrast	X	X	X	X	X	•				
arm style	X	X	X	236	X	X	•	X	X	
form	•	X	X	X	X	X				
midline	X	X	X	X	•	X	X	X		
x height	X	X	•	X						

ABCDEFG HIJKLMNO PQRSTUV WXYZ abc defghijklm nopqrstuv wxyz 123 4567890 .,;"&!?$

ITC Benguiat Gothic Medium 48 point

PANOSE abegmoqst

ITC Benguiat Gothic Book 24 point

PANOSE abegmoqst

ITC Benguiat Gothic Book Italic 24 point

PANOSE abegmoqst

ITC Benguiat Gothic Medium Italic 24 point

PANOSE abegmoqst

ITC Benguiat Gothic Bold 24 point

PANOSE abegmoqst

ITC Benguiat Gothic Bold Italic 24 point

PANOSE abegmoqst

ITC Benguiat Gothic Heavy 24 point

PANOSE abegmoqst

ITC Benguiat Gothic Heavy Italic 24 point

Supplier	**Alphatype CRS Digital Typesetter**
Usage	**Display, Text**
Similar Fonts	**Alphabet Soup, Cannot Moon**
Available Media	
Photo, Digital, DT, Bit	
Alternate Names	
Informal 851(BS)	

	1	2	3	4	5	6	7	8	9	0
serif	X	X	X	X	X	X	X	X	X	•
proportion	X	•	X	X	X	X				
contrast	X	X	X	X	X	•				
arm style	X	X	X	X	X	X	X	•	X	
form	•	X	X	X	X	X				
midline	X	X	X	•	X	X	X	X		
x height	X	X	•	X						

ABCDEFGH
IJKLMNOP
QRSTUVW
XYZ
abcdefghijkl
mnopqr
stuvwxyz
123456789
0.,;:''&!?$

Helios Rounded 42 point

ABCDEFGHIJKLMNO
PQRSTUVWXYZ
abcdefghijklmnopqrst
uvwxyz
1234567890.,;:''&!?$

Helios Rounded Light 24 point

**ABCDEFGHIJKLMNO
PQRSTUVWXYZ
abcdefghijklmnopqrs
tuvwxyz
1234567890.,;:''&!?$**

Helios Rounded Semibold 23 point

PANOSE abegmoqst

Helios Rounded Bold 24 point

Supplier	**Compugraphic 8400 Digital Typesetter**
Usage	**Display, Text**
Similar Fonts	**Formula One, Republic**
Available Media	
Hot, Photo, Digital	
Alternate Names	
Helios Rounded(CG)	

	1	2	3	4	5	6	7	8	9	0
serif	X	82	X	X	X	X	192	X	**232**	•
proportion	236	X	•	X	X	X				
contrast	X	X	X	X	X	•				
arm style	X	X	X	•	X	X	X	X	X	
form	•	X	X	X	X	X				
midline	•	X	X	X	X	X	X	X		
x height	X	X	•	X						

LIST OF SUPPLIERS

The following abbreviations for suppliers are used in the alternate names listing on the display pages. Much of the information used in the individual alternate names listing was provided by Frank J. Romano's book *The TypEncyclopedia*.

Adobe	*Adobe Systems (PostScript)*
Alpha	*Alphatype*
AM	*A&M Varityper*
Auto	*Autologic*
BH	*Berthold*
BS	*Bitstream*
CG	*Compugraphic*
CP	*Chart Pack*
Dymo	*Dymo, Photon Faces*
IBM	*International Business Machines*
Itek	*Itek Quadritek*
LS	*Letraset*
LSE	*Leonard Storch Enterprises*
Merg	*Mergenthaler Linotype*
Wang	*Wang Graphic Systems*

REGISTERED
TRADEMARKS

Every attempt has been made here to list all typeface names that are registered trademarks. Because the trademark status of some faces is somewhat murky, some trademarks may have been unintentionally excluded. The publisher should be notified if additions to this list are necessary.

ITC American Typewriter, ITC American Typewriter Condensed, ITC Avant Garde Gothic, ITC Avant Garde Gothic Condensed, ITC Barcelona™, ITC New Baskerville, ITC Bauhaus, ITC Benguiat, ITC Benguiat Condensed, ITC Benguiat Gothic, ITC Berkeley Old Style, ITC Bookman, ITC Caslon No. 224, ITC Century, ITC Century Condensed, ITC Cheltenham Condensed™, ITC Clearface, ITC Cushing™, ITC Elan, ITC Eras, ITC Esprit, ITC Fenice, ITC Franklin Gothic, ITC Galliard™, ITC Gamma, ITC Garamond™, ITC Garamond Condensed™, ITC Goudy Old Style, ITC Goudy Sans, ITC Isbell, ITC Italia, ITC Kabel, ITC Korinna, ITC Leawood, ITC Lubalin Graph, ITC Machine, ITC Mixage, ITC Modern No. 216™, ITC Newtext, ITC Novarese, ITC Quorum, ITC Ronda, ITC Serif Gothic, ITC Souvenir, ITC Symbol™, ITC Tiffany, ITC Usherwood™, ITC Veljovic™, ITC Weidemann™, ITC Zapf Book, and ITC Zapf International are registered trademarks of International Typeface Corporation.

Aldus, Auriga, Bernhard™, Bryn Mawr, Caledonia, New Calendonia™. Clarendon™, Cochin™, Corona, Egyptienne Frutiger™, Egyptian No. 505™, Eldorado™, Electra, Else™, Excelsior, Expert™, Frutiger, Glypha, Granjon, Helvetica, Helvetica Condensed, Helvetica Extended, Helventica Compressed, Helvetica Rounded, Icone™, Ionic 5™, Janson, Melior, Memphis, Meridien™, Metro™, Optima, Palatino, Peignot, Primer 54, Sabon, Spartan, Spartan Condensed, Syntax™, Times Roman, Trade Gothic, Trump™ Mediaeval, Versailles™, Video™, and Walbaum™ are registered trademarks of Mergenthaler Type Library.

Garth Graphic, Shannon, and CG Bem are registered trademarks of Compugraphic Corporation.

Antique Olive is a registered trademark of Foundries Olive.

Peignot, Unicia, and Univers are registered trademarks of Haas.

Accolade, Claridge, Congress, and Raleigh are registered trademarks of Ingramma.

Bramley, Brighton, Caxton, and Romic are registered trademarks of Letraset.

Bauer Bodini, Candida, Folio, Impressum, and Schneidler are registered trademarks of Neufville.

Brighton is a registered trademark of TSI.

Pasquale is a registered trademark of Tony Stan.

Adroit, Criterion, Heldustry, and Souvenir Gothic are registered trademarks of Typespectra.

Administer is a registered trademark of Typesettra.

BIBLIOGRAPHY

Biegleisen, J. T. *Handbook of Type Faces and Lettering*. New York: Arco Publishing, Inc., 1982.

Craig, James. *Designing with Type*. New York: Watson-Guptill, 1971.

Gates, David. *Type*. New York: Watson-Guptill, 1973.

Longyear, William. *Type and Lettering*. New York: Watson-Guptill, 1966.

Romano, Frank. *The TypEncyclopedia*. New York: R. R. Bowker, 1984.

Rosen, Ben. *Type & Typography: The Designer's Type Book*. New York: Van Nostrand Reinhold, 1976.

The Type Specimen Book. New York: Van Nostrand Reinhold, 1974.

Weinberger, Norman S. *Encyclopedia of Comparative Letterforms*. New York: Art Direction Book Co., 1971.

Supplier Specimen Books

Alphatype for the CRS Digital Typesetter

Compugraphic for the MCS 8400 Typesetter

Mergenthaler Library for the Linotronic 202 Typesetter

Mergenthaler Library for the Linotronic 300 Typesetter

CLASSIFICATION INDEX

ALPHABETICAL INDEX

Following is a list of all the font names that are found in this manual. The **bold** names designate the fonts displayed in the specimen pages. The nonbold names are referred to on the pages listed.

STYLISTIC INDEX

Following are frequently used font categories and the first digits of their classification numbers. Use the cross-reference charts from those pages to locate new variations of these familiar faces.

Century, 3233-
Clarendon, 3323-
Egyptian, 322, 331
Humanist Sans Serif, 911, 912, 913
Modern, 425
Old Style, 1121-
Sans Serif Condensed, 756
Serif Condensed, 152, 153
Slab Serif, 2167-
Swiss, 736
Transitional, 1133-
Typewriter, 466, 5567-, 866
Western, 2536-